Workarounds

50+ insider tactics for age 50+ entrepreneurs

By
Douglas Freeman
Ideascape, Inc.

Copyright ©2018; Revised edition
Douglas Freeman
Ideascape, Inc.
All rights reserved.

Printed in the U.S.A.

No part of this book may be reproduced or transmitted in any form or by any means, electronic or mechanical, including photocopying, recording or by any information storage and retrieval system, without written permission from the author.

ISBN: 1985785595
ISBN-13: 978-1985785595

DISCLAIMER

The author has made every effort to ensure that the accuracy of the information in this book was correct at time of publication. He does not assume and hereby disclaims any liability to any party for any loss, damage or disruption caused by errors or omissions, whether such errors or omissions result from accident, negligence or any other cause. Nothing written or implied in this book should be taken or construed in any way as legal or regulatory advice. The methods described in this book are the author's personal thoughts and those of his contributors. They are not intended to be a definitive set of instructions or professional advice. Inclusion of quoted experts shall not be interpreted as endorsements of their products and services. Readers should seek legal advice or other professional assistance with regard to business formation, licensing, regulations, accounting and legal document development.

DEDICATION

I dedicate this book to my hundreds of clients across the globe whom I've been honored to assist over nearly four decades. I also wish to thank my many colleagues in the communications, marketing, training and consulting businesses from whom I've learned so much. You've provided great inspiration to me. Thank you to the amazingly knowledgeable and talented experts who contributed their insights and advice to greatly enhance this book. And, I appreciate my many thousands of business connections and followers on business and social networks.

My father and mother were entrepreneurs, so I'm eternally grateful to them for providing unwavering support and being role models early in my career. Lastly, I dedicate this book to my wife and business partner, MacKenzie, who has coped with the ups and downs of being married to a lifelong entrepreneur.

TABLE OF CONTENTS

INTRODUCTION 1

PERSONAL AND PROFESSIONAL PAIN POINTS 7
1. Identifying What Business You're Really In 9
2. Figuring out What Your Brand Is 11
3. Committing to Your Entrepreneurial Venture 14
4. Doubting Your Professional Credibility 17
5. Framing Your Value as a Professional 20
6. Addressing Personal or Professional Baggage in Business 23
7. Getting Over Past Failures 25
8. Staying Relevant Professionally 28
9. Keeping Up to Date on Your Industry 31
10. Maintaining Work-Life Balance as an Entrepreneur 34
11. Asking for Help 37

BUSINESS OPERATION PAIN POINTS 41
12. Drafting a Workable Business Plan 43
13. Constructing a Marketing Action Plan 46
14. Developing a Marketing Resume and Capabilities Statement ... 49
15. Learning to Be Adaptable 52
16. Operating from a Home Office or Outside Office 55
17. Working Partly or Mostly In-house With Clients 58
18. Scaling Your Business 61
19. Establishing Contracts and Agreements 64

20. Formulating Your Rates 67
21. Packaging Your Services to Productize Them 70
22. Deciding Whether to Offer Discount Rates 73
23. Testing Niche Services to Penetrate a Market 76
24. Defending Against Income Volatility 79
25. Offering Alternatives to Payment for Cash-strapped Clients ... 83
26. Providing On-call Services 86
27. Managing Client Relationship Challenges 89
28. Controlling Client Interaction Time on Projects 92
29. Pitching Ideas to Clients 95
30. Working Remotely With Clients 98
31. Practicing the Right Level of Customer Service 101
32. Surviving Work Overload Periods 104

BUSINESS SUSTAINABILITY AND GROWTH PAIN POINTS 107

33. Seeking the Right Clients 109
34. Devising Ways to Make the Most of Referrals and Inside Tracks 112
35. Navigating the Paths of Resistance With Clients 115
36. Remembering the Power of Conversations to Build Your Business 118
37. Targeting the "Right" Types of Projects............................... 121
38. Spotting Hidden and Subtle Marketing Opportunities 124
39. Building an Effective Professional and Business Platform 127
40. Using Content Marketing to Build Visibility and Sell Your Services 130
41. Conducting Prospect Research to Increase Pitch and Proposal Success 133
42. Developing Proposals for Your Services 136
43. Selling Your Soft Skills Along With Your Expertise............... 141
44. Standing by Your Value Proposition 144
45. Pitching Services to Clients at Interviews and Meetings 146
46. Coping With Age Bias During Interviews 149

47. Completing Online Contract Applications 152
48. Engaging Matchmaking Agencies for Contract Work 155
49. Deciding to Use Online Freelancing Platforms 158
50. Competing to Win Contracts With Government Agencies 161
51. Using Project Wrap-Ups and Post-Mortems as Marketing Opportunities 164

FINAL THOUGHTS 167
52. Moving Beyond Pain Points to Success 169
53. Additional Advice and Insights From Experts Around the Globe 172
    About the Author 193

INTRODUCTION

Ageism exists in the work marketplace. That's the reality even though the Age Discrimination in Employment Act makes it illegal in the U.S. and there may be similar laws in other countries. Additionally, experience, knowledge and proven skills have been devalued in many industries and as a characteristic of the global economy.

Add to that the myths that most people age 50-plus are overqualified, too expensive, aren't creative or innovative, have out-of-date skills and aren't interested in learning new ones, aren't as productive as younger workers, won't be able to work effectively with younger managers and team members, are overly focused on "the way it's always been done," won't stay on the job very long, and won't "fit" with cultures in businesses and organizations today. This situation is aggravated when people age 50-plus often fail to employ all of the business development assets and resources they have from their work experience.

I'd love to cite useful statistics here to illustrate the scope of this issue, but reliable and meaningful data aren't available. One problem lies in definitions of self-employment titles. Terminology such as self-employed, microbusiness, small business, independent, freelance, gig, free agent, solopreneur, seniorpreneur, contractor, side hustle, contingent, part-time, temp and other descriptions are included, combined, excluded and interpreted differently within studies. It's also difficult to determine whether workers in these categories are committed long-term or not to self-employment. The research methods come into question, too. The populations used in many studies do not necessarily represent the broader population of the country studied. In other words, this is a subject that's very challenging to analyze due to many factors but also because what's generally called the freelance or on-demand economy is in a state of rapid change.

Therefore, I base my thinking on personal experience as someone who is age 50-plus and my research. I believe this gives me a reasonably good perspective on what's going on with careers of people age 50-plus.

I've found that a shocking number of my friends, colleagues and associates age 50-plus have been laid off from long-time employers. A high percentage of them have had great difficulty finding new jobs in their fields and at anywhere near the pay rates they've had in the past. I've had hundreds of conversations with these immensely talented people about their job-hunting experiences to add depth to the content of this book.

Many of their stories broke my heart. Far too many were unemployed, under-employed or felt like giving up on their careers. In addition to the emotional trauma they experienced was the personal economic impact. Very few of these people were in a position to retire—they wanted and needed income to get by. All of this is despite the fact that they have a wealth of knowledge, powerful skills, priceless experience and valuable networks of contacts. And this isn't just about the effects of this talent being under-utilized or wasted with these individuals. The negative economic impact of not having such talent in our workforce is enormous.

I've studied age 50-plus entrepreneurship over the last several years to understand the factors involved, trends and solutions people were finding to maintain their careers. Countless articles, blogs, videos, reports, studies, books and conversations later, I started writing about this subject on several online platforms. The feedback from the many thousands of readers about my posts and articles was enlightening, regarding the challenges they face in the job market. It was easy to conclude that people age 50-plus who want to continue their careers are looking for options outside of the traditional job market. That means they might consider self-employment as solo businesspeople or microbusinesses with partners or associates. I've come to believe that entrepreneurship is the best and, for many, the only career option.

This book is one of my efforts to do what I can to help fellow age-50-plus people become or remain successful in their entrepreneurial ventures. You see, I've been self-employed my entire career. This includes over three decades running my company Ideascape, Inc., as well as several other startups I co-founded. Having worked on contract (i.e. on-demand or freelance) with hundreds of private sector, government and non-profit clients, I've devised strategies and tactics to keep my business thriving and able to adapt to change. My experience plus that of many of my associates are the basis for the lessons learned and workarounds presented in this book.

This Workarounds Book

Age 50-plus entrepreneurs face unique challenges in the marketplace due to the issues I previously mentioned. I have no magical solutions to the problems they face in their self-employment ventures. I do offer what I call workarounds to the pain points we must confront to build sustainable and profitable businesses. The 52 workarounds are strategies and tactics that allow us to pivot around and avoid pain points. Think of them as lessons learned from a great many experiments I've tried, as well as advice from my circle of associates.

The independent businesspeople I've communicated with and I have used these workarounds successfully. This book's collection of strategies and tactics represent the most common pain points and associated workarounds. I hope they'll be useful to you no matter what field and industry you're in. I describe this book as a quick reference guide, because you can look up topics of interest in any order as your needs dictate.

I'm honored to be connected with some of the most brilliant experts on careers, career coaching and advising, age 50-plus businesses, "the future of work," entrepreneurship, and recruiting. They're based in over a dozen countries. Each has generously contributed their insights, lessons learned, advice and thoughts about the pain points and workarounds included in this book.

Each pain point appears as a separate topic, along with a conversation about its workarounds. I use the following terms to simplify the content in this book:

Associates – My friends, colleagues and network of business contacts in the U.S. and abroad, nearly all age 50-plus. This is a very diverse group with respect to job titles, fields of work, industries and sectors, as well as in characteristics ranging from education to ethnicity.

Professionals – You and all other self-employed businesspeople representing nearly every field and industry. You are a professional because you'll build or have built a long-term business, not just pursued a temporary work endeavor. Am I referring only to professions with licenses and certifications? No. I use the term professionals in a very inclusive way. These independent businesspeople represent just about every job description you can think of.

Entrepreneurs – You and all other self-employed businesspeople because you are the founders of your enterprises. Maybe you've heard it said that a freelancer or on-demand professional sells his or her hours, while an entrepreneur builds a business bigger than him or herself. In the case of 50-plus entrepreneurs, I propose that they combine these two definitions. They sell their hours but also look for ways to build passive income or a "bigger" business. They accomplish this by developing products related to their expertise (i.e. typically intellectual property), investing hours for stakes in clients' businesses and creating deep relationships with clients that could be a transferable business to a partner or merger with a similar firm.

Clients – Our customers.

Services – The focus of this book is on professionals who offer services, mainly because that's the type of business I know and the work most of my associates do. Certainly, a fair number of the pain points and workarounds also will apply to businesses that produce physical products.

Experienced – More than 15 years of professional work through previous employment or independent contracting.

Contracting or contractor – Independent businesses like ours work with clients on contract, which makes us contractors. Contracts are for single projects, multiple projects or defined periods of time.

Final Introductory Thoughts

Every day is a learning experience as an entrepreneur. The ground rules for business are changing at an increasingly rapid rate. Trends are being driven by technology, demographics, global business development and other factors. Many pain points associated with such pervasive change cannot be avoided. However, they can be addressed in ways to reduce their negative impacts or creatively used to the advantage of age 50-plus professionals. That said, I hope that the workarounds in this book will enhance your business strategies and spark effective actions to help fuel your success.

I also want to mention that there are many outstanding books, online courses, local classes, business startup consultants, Web-based information platforms, blogs and other resources available to you. I encourage you to explore these business tools to build on your strengths and improve in areas that may be holding you back.

Remember that you aren't alone in this journey of entrepreneurship. The age 50-plus demographic is collaborative, supportive, respectful and amazingly generous when it comes to assisting others. Together, over time, we can change how the business world values our potential and contributions.

PERSONAL AND PROFESSIONAL PAIN POINTS

1
Identifying What Business You're Really In

To name the business you're in seems so obvious, especially with your deep experience and skill sets. You're in the business of graphic design, insurance, financial management, motivational speaking, management consulting, executive coaching, product design or whatever. These are standard job descriptions for what you do in your business, right? Well, maybe. This is an unrecognized and underappreciated pain point for age 50-plus professionals.

For example, an associate of mine had been in the public relations (PR) business for many years, but wanted to move on to something new and more personally meaningful than PR. I asked him to describe the business he has been in. "Communications, publicity planning and strategizing, event management, promotion of clients to target media," he said. Certainly, those are functions in PR. But do they actually describe the business he has been in?

I asked him to consider looking at his work more globally. What's at the foundation? What about considering it from the perspective of the outcomes of that work? In general, he's a client visibility optimizer. At the foundation is that he's a connector and relationship builder. The outcomes include revenue enhancement, opportunity cultivation and credibility elevation.

The upshot was that his business could be defined more broadly than by his PR services alone. If he were to start his own business, it could be associated with PR but not be PR. For example, he's very talented at connecting people for mutually beneficial relationships. He could provide consulting services on successful networking techniques, create mixers or meet-ups to launch brain trusts, match professionals or businesses with complementary needs, speak to groups on developing business relationships, or blog on relationship building for a target audience such as startups. Yes, there really are companies and professionals who do all of these things. They're often categorized as marketing consultants even though there's far more to it than what would be defined as marketing.

As you launch your business venture, take some time to consider the business you're in from as many perspectives as you can. Disassemble the functions or elements of the general job description you're using. Go beyond those pieces to recognize particular talents you have that are associated with the activities common to your type of work.

There likely are more ways to use your skills and knowledge than you realize. And that new way of thinking might shape your business in a way that differentiates it from others and positions you to focus on functions you like the most.

Knowing what business you're in also can be integrated with your brand. Use that information to communicate your exceptional value to target audiences. Chances are this will set the stage for you to communicate your level of experience, knowledge and skills in a different way than before.

2
Figuring out What Your Brand Is

What's your brand? Marketing experts describe a brand as the image and substance you present via your messaging, Web site, printed materials, services and products, and communications. In many ways, it's how you operate and why you do it a certain way. Your prospective clients perceive your brand as your mission or personal cause for being in business, the value you offer, your quality and credibility, as well as what differentiates you from your competition.

This is a pain point for many of us who are age 50-plus. That's because it's easy to think of a brand being all about the type of business we're in and the marketing of a particular service or set of services. In some industries, brands are represented by nothing more than job titles. Generally, branding messages revolve around the applications of skills and knowledge of qualified professionals to solve customers' problems. Unfortunately, this doesn't do enough to differentiate businesses from their competition.

We could say that everyone from construction managers and trainers to writers and video producers all do the same work as others in their fields. The challenge with branding services like these is to establish ways to stand out and apart from everyone else. This helps you become visible to target prospects, become the professional to whom others refer their contacts and the one your desired prospects seek as the go-to person with solutions to their needs.

Because of your experience and all you have to offer your clients, you are the brand and no one is quite like you. Ideally, your story is one of integrity, maturity, deep knowledge, expert guidance, personal attention, passion, effectiveness, trustworthiness, resourcefulness and empathy. You are the professional whom clients want to hire and work with because of who you are, why you are in business, how you operate and the value you provide. Your brand is built on your story, which is core to the solutions you provide.

The name of your company or its pitch—perhaps even its slogan—reflects how you are different than others in your field. Your mission statement presents your unique approach to your business and what you strive to accomplish for clients. In all of your messaging you communicate your value within the context of your relationships with clients. One way to address all of this is to answer the following question: What makes your business especially meaningful to prospective clients?

For example, an element of my brand is reflected by my responsiveness to inquiries about my services. I do my best to call or write back quickly, even in cases when the project or prospect doesn't sound like a good fit. I'm also generous with my time and ideas during initial inquiries. This establishes an impression that shows how important it is to me to be available to my clients. I'm the professional my clients can count on to respond to urgent matters and be ready to collaborate immediately.

Understand that branding isn't stuff that you just make it up. Branding that works is all about authenticity. Customers can tell the difference between a brand that's authentic and one created just to sell or manufactured as a marketing device. Your customers are investing in you and the value of your experience, so they must see evidence of your brand in everything you say and do. Inconsistency is a credibility killer.

Here's an effective way to help you define or confirm your brand. If you've worked in an industry for a long time, it's likely that you've established a personal brand with colleagues and clients. It can be an enlightening experience to ask some of these people how they would describe your business or professional brand. You might even incorporate parts of their statements in your branding image and messages.

When developing your branding image and messages, just be sure to step back from thinking in terms of sales. Focus on the human side of what you do and what you're known for in your industry. Build a brand that attracts the types of clients you want to work with and the projects you desire.

3
Committing to Your Entrepreneurial Venture

If you're serious about building a successful business, I'm convinced that you need to be all-in. Your work is not a sideline, side job, gig, second job, moonlighting work, leisure pursuit or side hustle. You've decided to use your years of experience, skills, knowledge and ideas to create a sustainable business venture… or have you?

Just look at business social network profiles of deeply experienced people who proudly describe their own businesses. Then, look at their profile summaries. If they read like cover letter statements and resumes, chances are that those people are really looking for jobs rather than being fully committed to entrepreneurship. If everything pitches their experience, skills and knowledge within the context of their companies, then it's clear that they're committed to their own enterprise.

I've heard the following statement from a fair number of my associates: "I want to keep my options open in case someone wants to offer me a job with benefits." One associate is an accomplished professional who launched an online digital advertising training program a while back and was enjoying reasonable success. "I want to hedge my bets just in case things get rough on my own," she said.

This possibly-committed-but-I'm-not-sure approach is risky both ways. To prospective clients, she looks like she has set up a side venture and may or may not be around for an ongoing relationship. To potential employers, she appears to be someone who wants to be self-employed and might not stick around long at a job if things take off for her venture. Or, maybe both audiences conclude that her business is just something to fill in an employment gap and they're unsure which direction she wants to go.

This is a common pain point for us at this point in our careers. With entrepreneurship comes risk. There's also the out-of-pocket costs from having to fund our own benefits and business expenses. Employment, especially for long-time job holders, is attractive even if the work might not be so meaningful and there's a chance of being laid off at any time.

As an advocate for entrepreneurship, it should be no surprise that I'm all for making a 100% commitment to our business ventures. This simplifies our thinking, actions and authenticity when building our businesses. It reflects our confidence that we can successfully pursue our work. The only pain points are the ones we cannot prevent or avoid, which are part of entrepreneurship.

If commitment to your own venture is a pain point, I have a suggestion. Go all-in for a defined period, say one year. Align everything in your minimum viable business plan (explained later) to this time frame. Set milestones to measure your progress.

If your venture takes off quickly, then your decision to continue should be a non-issue. But as you near the end of that commitment period, objectively assess what you've accomplished and how your business is trending. Have the courage and confidence to keep pressing forward if there are promising indicators. Most importantly, be realistic about how long it takes to build a business like yours.

When you reach a point where you've lost confidence that your business will succeed, look for pivots to repackage and redirect your value proposition as another business. No one counts your failures. Everyone knows that's the way entrepreneurship works. Re-group, re-commit and move forward with the knowledge of what worked and didn't work.

If you decide to pursue a job in your career field, you already know how challenging that will be due to ageism and hiring trends within your industry. That's why I believe entrepreneurship is the best option for many of us, even if there are mis-steps and failures along the way. A failed business venture does not make you a failure. It really is a learning experience. The key is to use that knowledge to help you move on to your next venture.

4
Doubting Your Professional Credibility

"I feel like an imposter, not really the expert they think I am despite my years of experience." I've heard statements like this from colleagues when they were deciding whether or not to start their own businesses, as well as from even the most qualified businesspeople.

They've had self-doubts. I've had self-doubts. And chances are that you have too. It seems like a phenomenon that comes with the territory of being self-employed and an entrepreneur. No question, it's an especially big pain point for age 50-plus professionals to address.

The biggest problem with questioning your professional credibility, especially as a very experienced professional, is that hints of this self-doubt are exposed in proposals, pitches, communications with clients and prospects, Web site content, marketing content and conversations. Hints include being too quick to lower your fees or failing to sound confident about how you'll manage projects. Self-doubts can be reflected in how you say you'll address challenges, by minimizing your accomplishments and by hesitating when you describe your skill level and the value of your experience. Perceptions matter.

Those hints undermine your credibility with others. Companies hire contractors who are confident that they can successfully provide services and solutions. Any communications or behaviors that raise doubts in their minds put you at a disadvantage in being awarded and maintaining the contracts.

"Sometimes I feel like an old actor playing the role of an expert consultant in my field." That's what an associate once said to me. My first thought was to say how anyone involved in selling something relies on some acting skills. This hides our insecurities and fears. We can appear positive even when we're down.

Just look at great public speakers. They assume a role—albeit an authentic one—on stage, harnessing the power of silence, demonstrative movements and techniques of storytelling. In the same way, introverts must do their best to assume the role of extroverts to some degree to help them be successful entrepreneurs. Talk to actors who, when they take on a new role, very often doubt their ability to successfully portray the characters. They conjure up scenarios in which they'll lose the gigs and their careers will go down in flames.

The critical characteristic for businesspeople of any age is to be authentic and honest. Being a bit like an actor is not about being phony.

Every pitch, proposal and project involves the risk of failure just like any sales-oriented type of work. If we fail to win a few contracts in a row, we start questioning our professional credibility. That's despite the fact that we've got the skills, knowledge and experience equal to or better than our competition. We're qualified to do outstanding work for our clients and have the track record to prove it.

To address your credibility concerns, here are a few strategies I've used and picked up from my associates:

- Review your resume, CV or capabilities statement to remind yourself about the value you provide to clients you've served successfully.

- Make sure you have regular conversations with trusted colleagues, people who inspire you, those who tend to seek your advice and former clients to discuss what you do and the value you offer.

- Write down a description of the type of projects you'd enjoy most and how your skills, knowledge and experience could be applied successfully.

- Write a few short business cases for projects you've handled, along with the services you provided and the outcomes.

- Do a brief objective analysis of a contract opportunity you didn't win, including the factors that may have contributed to the failure and lessons learned from that experience.

These exercises will help remind you of your professional value that you've built over the years. This should help to minimize the pain point of feeling like an imposter when things go wrong.

5
Framing Your Value as a Professional

Discussions with my peers and especially with younger businesspeople often turn to questions about the professional relevance of those who are age 50-plus. This is a pain point we all should be prepared to address.

An associate who's a top corporate sales executive framed this situation perfectly at the conclusion of our discussion on the relevance question. He said that questions—and the associated biases and misconceptions—about the relevance of older workers is an opportunity to make a business case for hiring age 50-plus professionals as contract service providers. In other words, he likes to flip the discussion 180 degrees.

In the spirit of building that business case, here are some specific benefits we came up with that apply to professionals like us in a wide range of services and industries:

- Skills as a leader of people and organizations.
- Experience developing products and services, along with lessons learned in the process.
- Proficiency in marketing products and services, internally to stakeholders and externally to customers.

- Sensitivity and skills in being an advocate for customers and providing a high level of customer service.
- Experience with project management.
- Life experience in coping with adversity and success.
- Perspective about business trends, management philosophies and cultures.
- Experience with business, product and service life cycles.
- Skills related to forming and sustaining partnerships and alliances.
- Appreciation for responsive and value-based customer relations.
- Capability to analyze and identify valid evidence to evaluate products and services.
- Experience pitching startups and legacy businesses to strategic partners and investors.
- Understanding about business growth issues and solutions.
- Access to extensive networks of relevant contacts.
- Patience and perspective responding to change within organizations and in industries.
- Professional resourcefulness from business and life experience.
- Credibility within the industry or a related one.
- Cultural sensitivity from experience and values.
- Appreciation of loyalty and commitment.
- Understanding of the power of actions, not just talk.
- Knowledge about the value of planning and knowing that all plans are dynamic.
- Experience with failure and turning lessons learned into positive actions.

- Skills in collaborating with diverse teams.
- Capability to mentor clients with regard to institutional and industry knowledge and business skills.

This list should serve as a reminder to you about points you can make if you're in a situation that requires you to defend your relevance to your industry and prospective clients. However, the real value of these points lies in you relating them directly to your business profile. Match your skills, knowledge and experience with each point I listed to reframe your business relevance.

Career coaches and advisors often have their clients perform analysis exercises like this. The objective is to help their clients shape their business ventures and develop messages to convey during pitches and in proposals. It's also a way to remind their clients of what they have to offer in the marketplace from their long-time industry or work experience. Too often, we don't appreciate these value points unless we make an effort to explore them directly.

6
Addressing Personal or Professional Baggage in Business

By the time we reach the later stage of our careers, we've seen and done a lot in our work. There were good experiences and bad ones. We've developed our own biases and stubborn positions. Also, there are the limitations in skills or knowledge depending upon how well we've kept up with changes in our industry. All of this results in a major pain point especially common with those who are age 50-plus: personal or professional baggage.

Do we tend to overly rely on what we've done in past work and how we've done it? Do we have excuses for not keeping up on skills, knowledge, technology, industry trends, etc.? Do we have attitudes—preconceived notions and experience-rooted biases—about younger or less experienced colleagues and clients? Do we avoid types of projects or clients due to bad experiences with them in the past? Do we have a chip on our shoulder for whatever reason?

I warn my associates to dump the baggage or it'll be very challenging to succeed in a business. There's nothing wrong pursuing the types of clients, projects, working relationships and other preferences that fit your mission and business plan. However, negative attitudes and closed thinking can creep into marketing efforts and communications even with those prospects. These also affect your relevance in the marketplace.

As part of your business plan, you should note how you plan to remain relevant in the marketplace. Consider some training in your weak skills. Study trends in your field and industry to focus your services and tune into your niche(s). Become familiar with currently used communication, collaboration, project management and industry-specific tools. That way, you don't feel it necessary to mask your fading relevance with counterproductive attitudes or limitations on how you conduct your business.

Think of it this way, you're aiming to be hired because of the experience and solutions you have to offer. Those represent positive outcomes for customers. You must represent yourself as a professional who gets things done successfully to achieve those outcomes. There's no room for introducing negative messages or impressions in this proposition.

Sadly, I've heard stories from my clients about their negative experiences with professionals our age. They cite condescending communications, unwillingness to use current technologies such as collaboration and communication platforms, inflexibility with approaches to projects, and lack of interest in learning about industry trends affecting projects. Despite their qualifications for the jobs, this type of baggage was poison for the relationships.

There are plenty of pain points we face when building and maintaining our businesses as age 50-plus professionals. It's disadvantageous to add your own self-destructive baggage to the mix. Project the attitudes that you would look for if you were in your clients' shoes. This also will help you maintain your emotional health.

7
Getting Over Past Failures

I'd venture to say that every entrepreneur has experienced failure. This is a pain point that's part of the landscape even for the most successful businesspeople, especially for age 50-plus professionals with many years of experience.

This isn't to say that our entire business ventures often fail. Far more common is that particular marketing efforts or types of services just don't take off. Sometimes the market changes and we cannot compete any more. Clients pivot in ways that exclude us from their needs. There certainly are occasions when projects fail, through missteps by us or circumstances beyond our control.

If you've conducted adequate market research that has verified needs for your solutions for a category of client prospects and you are qualified to serve them, you should be able to build a successful business. This means you're able to package, price, present and deliver your services in ways that meet their needs.

Adjustments and adaptations always will be required to remain competitive. Yet, a total misread of the market or a big shift within it that no one could see coming might blow your entire business model out of the water. Based on the experiences of my network of associates, this isn't common because those years of experience and deep knowledge of their industries prompted them to prepare and plan well. The only times when their startups collapsed were when they didn't keep up with industry trends and centered their business models on "the way it's always been done" or other outdated thinking.

That said, I've found that my peers have a more difficult time coping with failures than when they were younger. "Look, when you're in your mid or late fifties or older and something big fails, you don't have lots of time to restart with the same energy or conviction," an associate said to me.

I'd argue that this attitude about failure can be shifted. First, many of us have no choice other than entrepreneurship. Therefore, a failure must be taken as a temporary setback. The lessons learned will be used with the next incarnation of that business or a different one. There could be instances when what seems like an unrecoverable failure actually is a sign that a solo business isn't a great fit for you. That's when your pivot may be to find the right partnership to establish, even if the business is different than what you tried alone.

Very often, the difference between those who ultimately succeed and those who give up is resiliency. It's the ability to learn from failures and setbacks. They use that knowledge to set out in a different direction or use the experience in a positive way. Failures are information, feedback. They aren't personal indictments on you or your value.

Self-employment is a journey of course adjustments while conducting your business. As an experienced but nimble entrepreneur, you're positioned to experiment continuously and aggressively. Succeed or fail fast. Failing fast means that you don't sink your business by sticking with an unsuccessful effort too long. There should be a point where you can step back, evaluate what you're doing and decide if it makes business sense to proceed longer, make adjustments or ditch the effort.

There's no magical formula for determining which action to take. I suggest that you examine milestones and make a thoughtful business case for which path to choose. Failing or encountering setbacks is not fun. It's easy to become frustrated and wonder if you'll find the right formula to build a sustainable business in the years ahead.

However, with resiliency you can navigate your way through setbacks to end up accomplishing great things. Be pragmatic. Prepare, strategize, act, succeed or fail, learn, move forward with improvements, and repeat. This is the path to coping with the pain points of failures as best you can, so you can focus on building the business you envision.

8
Staying Relevant Professionally

Like any professional, you need to dedicate time and effort to stay relevant to your client market. This means you must stay current with the skills necessary for the market's needs and knowledge about developments and trends in your industry. If you don't keep up, you're risking the catastrophic pain point of obsolescence.

This is an especially big risk for age 50-plus professionals. One of the most common generalizations about us is that we don't have the skills and knowledge to address today's issues. Unfortunately, there's truth to this judgement as there are many of us who don't have the motivation to keep up or learn new skills.

An example of keeping up regards using collaboration platforms. These platforms are used to manage aspects of contractors' projects, employing everything from calendars and shared documents to conference calls and relationship management. If you aren't familiar with these tools, you'll be presenting a barrier to getting hired. These are the tools your prospective clients may use—ones they expect you to be comfortable using.

Your skills likely need to be enhanced on an ongoing basis, especially in industries where certifications or special technologies are required to perform work. The nice thing is that you can find training for almost anything online. If not, be sure to keep up on trends and take any available courses as necessary. A good source for direction and offerings in this area is your professional organization. I've had outstanding learning experiences through meetings, presentations, workshops and conferences via several organizations.

Many of my associates report great value in attending conferences all over the country. They feel this is an efficient way to stay current on skills, knowledge and trends. It also affords them opportunities to network with colleagues and prospects. Some invest their time and money to build connections and familiarity with certain events to set themselves up as future speakers or panelists.

Attending conferences can be quite costly, so I suggest that you choose strategically. I consider conferences that provide solid training through workshops on trending skills or topics, networking opportunities with target clients, the chance to meet prominent experts in my field, and ideally visit a location where I can conduct other business activities.

Relevance also is about staying ahead of the curve. Sometimes you can recognize trends in your field and industry by reading, through conversations with people in and outside your field, and by listening to clients. It's easier to just keep up than to position yourself a step ahead. Therefore, you must ask the right questions to a diverse group of individuals at the right times to anticipate change and opportunities.

An effective way I've found to become aware of trends within my industry and those that potentially could affect my industry is through startups. I follow startup developments online via news or notification services. I'm constantly asking: What's going on here? How could the activities of these startups affect an aspect of my industry? And, how could what these startups do affect my target clients? Then, I ask how I can move in those directions with my services, network development and marketing.

Additionally, I engage with startup founders and teams through networking and outreach efforts to them as potential clients. An advantage I have is that my services apply to all industries and sizes of organizations, so connections are relatively easy to make. But, this approach can work within any type of service. While I'm providing services to startups, I'm also asking plenty of questions and making many observations to learn from those interactions.

I really want to stress the importance of staying relevant to our markets. It's easy to be lazy and assume that the skills and knowledge we've used for a long time are just as valuable today. In certain cases and with some capabilities we have, that's true. I wouldn't bank on that, though.

Just start a conversation about your business with someone much younger working in your field. If you don't understand some of the lingo, have never heard of the companies referenced, haven't had any experience with technologies mentioned or aren't aware of the issues brought up, you have some serious work to do to get up to speed. Your business survival depends on it.

9
Keeping Up to Date on Your Industry

You don't know what you don't know. And what you don't know can mean opportunities are lost. The pain point for us is figuring out how to keep up our professional skills, but also with our industries and developments outside our industries that may affect our work or market for our services.

I keep up with news and trends within my profession and industry in several ways. It's amazing how informative posts are from industry colleagues on social networks. I'm fortunate to have a large network of contacts who regularly share valuable information, insights, observations and news. I'm also a member of a special interest groups on social networks, representing a broad number of fields. Scans of members' posts yield informative content that's relevant to my work and interests.

For general profession related news, I subscribe to several daily, weekly and monthly news and information reports. Sources are from industry or sector related publications, companies, business organizations, specialized journalists, educational institutions, and subject matter experts.

What should you and I look for? This depends on the pain points you need to address to keep up as an informed professional. The basic takeaways should be news and information that support your skills and knowledge. This is content that makes you feel confident that you know what's going on in your business world, but also motivates you and inspires ideas. For example, you must keep up on trends related to projects you tend to seek and the types of clients you want to pursue. What do you need to learn to understand the current needs of prospective clients? What should you know to be able to have meaningful conversations with colleagues and clients?

The other key action is to define your prospective clients' needs by asking a broad range of marketing questions. Where is your future work going to be coming from? What are the developments that will best help you adapt to changing market conditions and directions of your clients' industries are headed? What are emerging pain points for your prospective and current clients? What opportunities are arising from prospective clients just outside the traditional circle of businesses in your industry?

If you want to or already serve a specific group of companies or organizations, you should keep up on them. Use news search utilities or RSS feeds for online publications to provide you with alerts when articles or news releases are published. I automatically receive summary reports that contain headlines and links to sources on companies. Searches are based on key words or phrases that are relevant to my marketing efforts. Also, you can "follow" companies on many social networks to receive their news, articles and posts.

When I run across news or information that is actionable, I usually do a bit more research to figure out what steps I can take. In some cases, I'll note a contact to follow up with to see if they can use my services. I use other alerts as prompts to devise strategies to reach out to or connect with new markets or prospects. Additionally, some news or information helps me know what to follow for future investigations and marketing actions.

I check my email, news and social network resources daily for valuable information. Over the years, I've cut down the number I receive due to quality, relevance and timeliness of the content. I also add new sources as they come to my attention.

It's critical to stay on top of this effort because you don't want these messages to pile up and become an overwhelming task to address. Don't set yourself up for information overload. Try starting with only a handful of sources that seem to be the most valuable and clearly related to your profession and industry. Add a few in more general sources that offer a bigger picture of interesting news and trends.

Only you can determine what's necessary to know to keep your business thriving. Your goal is to position yourself on the leading edge in your field by keeping up as a professional as well as staying aware of broader market opportunities.

10
Maintaining Work-Life Balance as an Entrepreneur

A well-crafted work and life balance offers age 50-plus professionals a rewarding and meaningful journey. Often, there are pain points along the path to that destination. Some factors are in our control, while others are not.

Even if you have on-call contracts that provide a relatively steady stream of projects coming your way, there's always a need to complement those with additional projects. That creates unpredictable occasions of heavy workloads and circumstances when evening and weekend work is necessary to fulfill obligations.

I've had the full range of experiences over the years. Some lessons were learned the hard way about maintaining a work-life balance. That balance has ranged from bordering on unhealthful disruption to ideal, with nicely acceptable or better situations being the norm as my career progressed.

When we experience dry spells with work, we definitely can feel the stress. There's a reflex to spend long hours marketing, networking and re-evaluating our current services. Stress results from questioning our niche and the long-term demand for our services. When this situation turns into a daily frenzy or negative feelings erode our confidence, the balance shifts in a bad direction and our quality of life suffers.

If you have a home office, there can be a temptation to work all the time. Deadlines loom, ideas come to mind that draw you in to do a little work here and there, and clients call during off hours due to emergencies. On-call contracts can really throw off normal work hours, especially with those end-of-the-day requests to take care of some work to deliver the next morning. You feel responsible to provide outstanding service and fulfill commitments on projects, so you do the professional thing and get the job done. It's not a choice many times. This is part of what self-employment is all about.

During times when our workload exceeds our comfort zone, our work-life balance can get out of whack. Long hours in evenings and on weekends can lead to burnout. That's as risky to our health as the stress of not having enough work. There's a tendency to not eat right, get proper exercise, take enough breaks and maintain healthy relationships with loved ones and friends.

The number one rule for solo entrepreneurs to succeed is to take care of yourself. Your marketing, work and life will suffer if you don't commit to maintaining a work-life balance. Yes, there will be spells when you push the boundaries. The key is to force yourself to follow the routines that support a healthful balance. I know it's easier to talk about being disciplined with the issue of balance than to actually do it, but I can't emphasize enough how important this is to sustain a successful business.

If work overloads occur too often and cannot seem to be prevented, you might consider establishing a partnership or small group of subcontractors. Off-loading pieces of projects that don't require your expertise can be a lifesaver. Also, you might consider outsourcing some business tasks that take time but don't really need to be done by you. My associates often outsource accounting, basic types of research, aspects of project record-keeping, marketing content writing and posting, Web site maintenance and initial inquiry responses.

One of the best things I do when experiencing stressful downturns in work is to increase the number of conversations I have with trusted colleagues and other business contacts. This counteracts feelings of isolation which tend to compound negativity and frustration. The intellectual stimulation and positivity of these interactions build confidence and spark new ideas. All of this reminds me that persistence, resourcefulness and confidence in my value always lead to good outcomes.

There is nothing more important than maintaining a healthful work-life balance. Find the formula that works for you and make a commitment to take care of yourself as you build or sustain a thriving business.

11
Asking for Help

When was the last time you asked for help with something related to your work? I've gotten way too many blank stares from associates when I asked them this question. Their excuses? "I don't want to appear that I don't know what I'm doing" or "If I'm so knowledgeable, I should be able to figure things out myself."

This is a pain point that's common with age 50-plus professionals because we feel we should have all the answers due to our level of experience. I've been fortunate to have an amazing network of associates who serve as a sort of brain trust. We bounce questions or issues off each other to gain fresh perspectives and advice.

For example, one associate of mine was questioning his plan to launch a niche consulting business. Even writing out a basic business plan didn't seem to give him enough confidence in his concept. He asked me for my "brutally honest opinion." Instead of starting with my gut feelings about whether this work appeared to be a good fit for him and if there'd be a market for his services, I asked him a series of questions. The questions pertained to details about the business and market, but I also posed several scenarios of situations that could occur in this work. He articulated responses smoothly and confidently with the passion of a very credible professional. Obviously, this business was a great fit for him in every way and I told him so.

When addressing big questions regarding career changes or new business directions, you might consider enlisting help from a career or business coach. I have many associates who have hired coaches and advisors. Most have said that it worked best if the coaches had some understanding about their industry or type of work. They also found it easy to ask for help this way because these are trained and often certified professionals in the business of providing such guidance.

How about getting a mentor? Age 50-plus professionals may find it awkward to seek a mentor to rely on for help. We're typically the ones in that role. I've known plenty of people who have benefited greatly from mentors but that was when they were starting off in their careers. It could be challenging to find someone who could assume a traditional mentorship role for us at this stage of our career. A place to start might be your professional organization or by approaching a top author or speaker in your field. Perhaps your offer could be to establish a peer-to-peer mentorship for a mutually beneficial relationship.

A new twist on mentorships is for older and younger individuals to advise or guide each other as co-mentors. The mix of experience levels, generational perspective and niche expertise can result in beneficial relationships. Guidance available through these co-mentorships might be limited to certain work areas due to age and experience, though. Places to look for candidates include startup incubators, MBA programs and co-working spaces.

As I said, I have a small network of trusted associates to help me out from time-to-time. We communicate by email, phone calls and chats over coffee sometimes. I'd say phone calls are the most common. There's nothing formal about this group. You could pitch the idea of starting a group like this to just a few contacts and let it evolve and expand organically. Maybe agree to schedule a conference call, email exchange or meeting each month. Otherwise, just propose that you all be available to help each other as needed.

A final pain point regards feeling comfortable asking for help. What helped me get over the awkwardness of asking for help was to be very specific with my questions and frame them appropriately for the particular associate.

For example, a question could be asked like this, "I've been struggling with [fill in the situation or problem] and I'd like to get your thoughts about how you would handle it." It's usually better to frame your question so that you gain their insights on the challenge rather than directly asking for advice about what you should do. Few people want to assume that responsibility. But asking what they would do allows them to put themselves in your shoes to suggest an approach.

BUSINESS OPERATION PAIN POINTS

12
Drafting A Workable Business Plan

I'm always amazed at how many solo and micro businesses run by very experienced people don't have even basic workable business plans. These would be plans that address their branding, business focus and services, marketing, and business case for existing. Experienced businesspeople should know better.

They have many excuses. The most common one is that they aren't sure what goes into a business plan and want to focus on "doing," more than on planning. Rarely do they want to spend precious funds to pay for assistance in developing a plan. There's also an impression that a business plan must be this elaborate study as would be required for an investor.

Guess what? You are the investor in your business—with time, money and resources. If you'd want to examine a business plan for a new venture before investing money in it, why wouldn't you want the same for your own business?

I propose a simple compromise by using the lean startup methodology. A key approach within its framework is to create minimum viable products (MVPs). An MVP often is a bare-bones first version of a product to test with prospective customers. If it solves a problem effectively—there's a need for it—you build a more complete version to make a business of it. If it doesn't resonate with prospective customers, you've failed fast. This prevents risking everything and investing a huge amount of time on one idea with little chance of success. The same process applies to services, not just physical products.

This is an effective approach to develop a business plan for a business like yours, considering the fact that you are the product for your venture. A minimum viable business plan addresses the key pain points in conceptualizing and operating your business. To draft a minimum viable business plan is not an overwhelming or highly complex project to undertake.

An important thing to remember is that you aren't committing to a permanent plan that dictates all you do in your business. It's a flexible, adaptable presentation of your business and what you'll do—a living document that will change as you make your way forward. This plan doesn't need to be perfect nor all-inclusive. *Minimum viable* are the operative words here.

In one or two pages, your plan should simply and clearly explain your branding, business niche, services, pricing, initial marketing activities and the opportunity or need for your services. This is so you know where you're heading with your business. Additionally, many entrepreneurship experts suggest that you include your desired monthly or annual income goal so that you have a target in mind.

I'm reminded of a consulting company I co-founded with a partner I had known and respected for years. We identified a niche that we were qualified to pursue due to our experience, skills and connections. Even though we crafted a rough description of our services for our Web site, we opted not to write a business plan. You might say it was a minimum viable company—an experiment. Due to this and some enticing opportunities, we took our chances launching before clearly thinking through what we were doing and putting that in a plan.

During a pitch to a prospective client, it became obvious that we hadn't settled on the details about the services we would provide. We lacked clear explanations about our unique process and the expected outcomes. A minimum viable plan would've prevented this situation or made us re-think starting the company.

A big advantage of writing down the elements of your business plan is that it makes you think through your business concept and what you anticipate doing to make it work. The fact is that, as age 50-plus professionals, we have less time for false starts and overly long business growth cycles. It may be a pain point to write a business plan, but it'll prevent many worse pain points down the road.

With each element of your plan, keep asking yourself why it makes good business sense. Be a critic, but one who is willing to accept some unknowns, a reasonable level of risk and experiment in new directions.

13
Constructing a Marketing Action Plan

A minimum viable business plan should address your marketing strategy in at least a bare bones manner. However, you need a more detailed marketing action plan to ensure that you're organized as you continually promote your business. This includes marketing experiments as well as updates to your strategy.

Developing and using a marketing action plan is a common pain point for age 50-plus professionals. The reason is that we often rely on our instincts and habits to guide our actions. It takes a more strategic approach these days to navigate the many barriers we face when marketing ourselves, including the rapidly changing marketplace for our services. A thoughtfully constructed marketing action plan can increase the efficiency of your marketing activities.

What does a typical marketing action plan contain? Think of this as a priority list in two sections. One section is a list of perhaps five to 10 major marketing efforts that span six months to a year, listed from highest priority to lowest. Just because an effort is ranked lower doesn't mean it's not important to address. The only marketing efforts on this list are ones that must be acted upon during this time frame.

For example, efforts might include using content marketing on specific social networks. The objective is to reach out to certain target prospects to increase your visibility, attract incoming inquiries and open communications that might identify business opportunities.

For each of your major marketing efforts, you should complete the second section with daily or weekly actions to support those efforts. These are your to-dos or checklists to ensure continuity of your marketing, during slack times and even busy times.

For example, actions listed under content marketing could include posting one original article and two brief posts per week. These should be developed from a content production idea list that you maintain, which is expanded as your reading or work sparks ideas that you note for reference. Perhaps you aim to research and pursue one speaking engagement each week from your frequently updated list of future conferences and industry or professional organization events. To-do items might include emails or calls to organizers as well as submission of proposals.

Also, you might chip away daily at target company contact lists to get referrals for projects, submit introductory pitches to prospective clients using target lists or complete proposals for prospects you've had communication with previously. It's likely that a fair portion of your daily or weekly marketing time will be researching prospective clients and networking with contacts so opportunities to take specific marketing actions are revealed.

How you track your marketing actions to keep up on the status of each depends on what works best for you. Many of my associates use customer relationship management software or their own databases to accomplish this. I've tried several of these tools and each has its advantages and limitations. What works best for me these days is a simple word processing table because I have very focused marketing efforts. This is linked to a contact database to record all company names, position titles, email address, phone numbers, Web sites, etc.

Typical information to record includes the following: contact identification and communication information, how and why you connected with the person, dates for all interactions, notes about interactions including marketing action details, reminder dates for follow-ups, and ideas for further networking or marketing that may or may not relate specifically to this person.

The goal of a marketing action plan is to ensure that you work efficiently, continuously and purposefully over time. That said, this plan must be adaptable as changes are called for due to trends in results and especially from unanticipated opportunities.

Flexibility in sticking to your plan is crucial. I've had to drop everything at times to take on an emergency project, compose a proposal for a time-sensitive opportunity and contact prospects from referrals immediately because of opportunity windows. As soon as possible, I catch up on missed action plan items. It's important not to fall behind on marketing efforts or work gaps can sneak up on you.

14
Developing a Marketing Resume and Capabilities Statement

What's the difference between an independent business professional's marketing resume and that of a job hunter? Both appear to market an individual's skills, knowledge and experience for certain types of work within the scope of a defined role.

The differences may seem subtle, but these really are two very different marketing pieces. A pain point is that most people are more accustomed to developing job resumes than business marketing resumes.

As an independent business professional, you are pitching your credentials for a single project or series of projects typically over a set period. You aren't presenting an argument for what a valuable long-term employee you would be, how you'd work for a company exclusively, grow with their enterprise and potentially move up within their ranks. You're pitching a business entity that serves many clients in multiple ways.

Compensation, work processes, responsibilities and other relationship characteristics are quite different for outside professionals than for employees. In other words, your business model is completely different than that of someone looking for a job. Marketing resumes essentially present a business case for someone with your professional assets.

In my experience contracting with companies and government agencies, most don't ask for resumes as a starting point for consideration. They've been referred to me, they've checked my Web site, reviewed my social media profiles or they've previously had some type of communication with me. Therefore, most have expected my credentials or qualifications to be included as a section in proposals. They don't necessarily care about my complete work history. What they want is my work history that's relevant to the specific project they have. This would be my track record working on similar projects and maybe with similar types of organizations. Just as no two proposals I draft are the same, the resume sections are rarely the same.

I've found success using marketing resumes that include descriptions of projects presented like very brief case studies. These included the name of the client, work or problem I addressed, how I provided solutions, which skills were used, and the final outcomes of my work. Subtly, it markets the benefits of that client hiring me. All of this is highly customized for relevance to the prospective client, the nature of the project and the skill set I'm marketing. The level of detail in each case presented depends on whether the work was covered by a non-disclosure agreement (NDA)—the information is generalized as necessary if an NDA applies.

It seems that nearly all online contract job platforms require submission of a resume for profiles. Some can automatically pull information from your social network platform profiles. This process can be unreliable due to the type of information your profile contains and how you structure the presentation of it there.

Part of the reason for job platforms' reliance on resumes is that they're stuck in the employment (job) model. They don't understand the differences between employment and business-to-business marketing, nor the nuances of how contracting decisions are made.

A great alternative to dependence on resumes is a capabilities statement. Essentially, the business version of resumes are capabilities statements. I've found these to be quite useful in my marketing efforts, especially when seeking contracts with government agencies and large corporations.

A capabilities statement is a one-page presentation of your business emphasis, core competencies, list of clients, business achievements and awards, professional associations, licenses and accreditations, and business classification categories (e.g., NAICS codes). Most often, I've used general purpose versions focused on a specific type of service or group of services. There have been occasions when I customized this document for particular prospects and types of contracts to emphasize certain credentials or experience.

Capabilities statements are great to attach to initial inquiry responses as well as with proposal submissions. You might even consider including a downloadable version on your company Web site as a marketing tool, if appropriate for your services and prospects.

When it comes to marketing resumes, our years of experience as evidenced by our work history is the basis for our value proposition. Good marketing resumes and capabilities statements include information that shows how we've kept our skills up to date and added new ones, expanded our knowledge, worked with younger people and new companies, and have used current communication and technology tools. These tools are proof that we're relevant and valuable as contract professionals. They support the business case for hiring us for projects.

15
Learning to Be Adaptable

The future of work and careers for age 50-plus professionals is… disconcerting and an ongoing pain point. Changes in the scope of job functions, where work is conducted, how work is performed and the ways that workers are managed are being re-imagined daily. The nature of work itself is changing.

So how do you plan for the unplannable for your business to survive and thrive? Maybe you don't. Perhaps you're better off asking a different question: How do I shape my career at this point to adapt to constantly changing work and economic conditions? Yes, it's all about your adaptability to address this pain point.

I've always been inspired by associates who have sustained adaptable, entrepreneurial careers for decades. Their interests and curiosity, new opportunities, changes in the marketplace, and client requests guided their career transitions. In my case, these same influences changed what I did through my company, resulted in co-founding startups and even provided chances to acquire equity in another entrepreneur's venture.

I've accomplished this via continuing education, plenty of reading, more listening than talking, experimentation in new fields, being alert to opportunities, as well as acceptance of some risk and failure. I firmly believe that we must adopt entrepreneurial style and adaptable careers to succeed.

There are many benefits from positioning yourself for an adaptable career to spot opportunities and operate at the forefront of trends. How many of the following actions are you taking regularly?

1. Reading about trends and developments within and on the fringes of your current industry and areas of expertise.
2. Listening to colleagues, influencers, friends, network contacts, clients and leaders inside, as well as on the periphery, of your profession and industry to pick up on emerging needs.
3. Building your creative and critical thinking skills through self-directed or other training.
4. Preparing yourself to be resourceful when it comes to problem-solving and maneuvering around barriers, especially those unique to age 50-plus professionals.
5. Consistently adding new skills to enhance your ability to successfully pursue opportunities.
6. Interacting with and expanding your business network to position yourself for referrals, references, offers and advice.
7. Experimenting with your career by testing new interests in different ways within and outside your areas of expertise.
8. Building your personal brand and marketing yourself or your business to prepare for lost clients, evaporating contracts and shifting marketplaces.
9. Developing a flexible mindset when it comes to your career so that even if you find work that you love to do, you are devising ways to make it align with future changes.

10. Asking probing questions about your own and industry assumptions, the relevance of your expertise, the future of your clients, etc. to prevent wondering, "Why didn't I see that coming?" in the future.

Making your career more adaptable requires personal commitment and an ongoing series of small actions. There's great value in adopting a startup style entrepreneurial mindset, because you are the product and service competing for relevance in the changing marketplace.

Adaptability will help you thrive in the chaotic intersection of work and careers that will be the norm from now on.

16
Operating From a Home Office or Outside Office

I've been asked countless times how I can get anything done working from a home office. People are astounded that I've been doing this for nearly my entire career, although there have been short stints working part-time on-site at clients' offices. A home office works for me and the businesses that I'm in, mainly because most of my services can be provided remotely so clients rarely visit my office.

The decision to use a home or outside office can be a pain point for many, especially those who have had long careers in corporate offices. They're just accustomed to working in an office environment. Yet, a big issue for self-employed professionals is that offices can be costly. That overhead expense may be an undesirable cash-flow challenge, especially when starting out. If all of your work is performed remotely, you may not need an office. That is, as long as you have the discipline and control over distractions at home to work efficiently.

If the nature of your work requires meetings with clients on your turf, a separate office of some type probably is best to maintain a professional image. In cases when your work involves physical products, again, you might need to have office and storage space outside your home.

If you've formed a business with a partner or two and want to work together, I'd say an office space is wise. That will maintain your privacy, prevent city zoning or other residential restriction violations, and avoid some liabilities associated with a multi-person operation in your home.

One option is for you to start off working from home and transition to an outside office as needs dictate and finances allow. I know plenty of professionals who have done this. A hybrid approach might be to combine a home office with a virtual office. That provides an address, virtual or live receptionist, communication services, and meeting rooms—some offer co-working spaces or offices that are available via reservations.

Your options for office space vary widely, depending on where you're located. Metropolitan areas tend to offer the most possibilities. For example, a traditional small office in an office building may be a first choice especially if there will be client visits. This may be the most expensive choice, though. Executive suites, with a shared receptionist and other facilities, are a less expensive option for many professionals I know. Also, there are shared offices that are a bit like short-term timeshares where you reserve use of a space with one or two other businesspeople.

Startup facilities and incubators can be viable options if your business fits their "work community" design. These tend toward businesses such as tech, consumer products and product design.

Co-working spaces have become attractive to a wider range of businesses than when they originally focused nearly exclusively on tech startups. Their facilities range from permanent separate office spaces to individual workstations and meeting rooms that rent by the hour.

Startup facilities and co-working spaces often are populated by younger entrepreneurs. This can create opportunities for older professionals, such as consulting, mentorship and advisory board invitations. On the negative end, they can be a challenging cultural fit and age discrimination can be disheartening.

Another option is a public space such as a coffee shop, café, library or public college campus. Public spaces may be useful as temporary workplaces, due to the advantages of being free and there's the energy of other people being around. However, Wi-Fi usually isn't secure and phone calls may be awkward for privacy.

Certainly, a pain point of working alone in a home office is the isolation. Any type of traditional shared or co-working office space offers its own business ecosystem inhabited by others. That allows for spontaneous interactions with people in all types of businesses. Some office buildings coordinate events or provide gathering spaces to foster new relationships among resident businesspeople. Co-working and startup type facilities are well known for offering opportunities for member interaction.

Deciding whether to work at home in a dedicated space or in an outside office really depends on personal preferences, your type of business and the affordability of outside office space. You might ask others in your field to learn from their experiences. It's an important business decision, so think strategically and in line with your work style.

17
Working Partly or Mostly In-House With Clients

Ready to work with a client in-house? It depends on your types of services and industry whether any contracts will specify in-house work. "High touch" services such as training, coaching, on-site research, change management, project management and some types of software programming and product design often require working face-to-face with staff or using company facilities.

In-house work can present some pain points for age 50-plus professionals, though. Two common ones my associates and I have faced are company culture and productivity. By company culture, I mean collaborating effectively often with much younger teams and unconventional work styles shaped by the type of business they're in. This especially seems to be the case with tech startups and niche product creators.

Productivity issues relate to influences that affect your time management. In many organizations, there's a tendency for contractors to be obligated to attend an excessive number of meetings. Also, there are non-project related distractions by team members who see age 50-plus professionals as mentors as well as subject matter resources for advice outside the contractual scope of work.

To address the company culture challenge, the most common approach we've used is to constantly steer the focus of interactions back on the projects rather than engage on attitudes related to age. We emphasize the expertise we have and why we were hired. Some employees might discount the value that older contractors offer or feel threatened in some way by this outside expert "invading" their workplace. This friction can be diffused by us ramping up our efforts as team players with positive attitudes and respectful approaches. A most powerful factor that aided smooth integration into cultures was achieving successful results for our work.

Productivity issues are a bit more challenging for in-house contractors. There are no magical solutions to the meeting problem. Managers often want to make sure the contractor feels included. This may be because the topics discussed at meetings could be relevant to the project and his or her perspective could be valuable. The best defense can be to bring up the project's pressing schedule requirements and the possible additional cost of extra meetings, adding to the scope of work.

Other common distractions are quick chats for feedback or ideas and employees wanting the contractor to "just take a look" at something. These could only be minimized by citing the fact that our contracts don't allow us to veer outside our scope of work. The reality is that most of us end up helping out employees to be nice and build relationships. That's fine as long as our productivity isn't affected so much that our work suffers.

I've only had a handful contracts that required significant in-house work, mostly with a large federal agency. In those experiences, the functions I performed actually did need to occur in their offices. Maybe because there was a very diverse staff—in age and areas of expertise—I had no cultural barriers to deal with. Although there were some characteristics of government bureaucracies to adapt to as well as the typical challenges of working with highly specialized or technical professionals.

Fortunately, there was great respect for my services and the specific projects I was responsible for, so there were few distractions. Some of the requests to take a look at something or to get my thoughts on a subject ended up turning into invitations to work on new projects, so that ended up being a benefit.

Many of my associates have had similar stories about how in-house work nurtured relationships in ways that remote work couldn't. Those contracts resulted in other in-house work as well as contracts for remote work. Most often, the new projects were similar to the original ones. This makes sense due the dynamics of working closely with teams and contributing to successful outcomes for projects. Trust and positive results are powerful marketing influences.

Maybe the lesson learned from my experience and I'm sure that of my associates is that it can be worth seeking some in-house work. It's an effective way to build lasting and profitable relationships with clients. They come to realize the value you have to offer and issues regarding age become irrelevant.

18
Scaling Your Business

There are several ways to address the pain point of a need to scale your business while staying true to your professional goals at this stage of your life. By goals, I mean a desire to operate alone or with only one or two partners.

My associates and I have used one or more of the following approaches: alliances, joint ventures, partnerships, subcontracting and co-ops. We did this to expand our service offerings, increase credibility to target markets, propose strong teams for contract opportunities, pursue special ventures due to shared interests and create businesses to test market specific services or products.

Due to our years of business experience, we likely know which options fit best with our work-styles and preferences. All of these options have advantages but also their own pain points. I've used all of these scaling methods, except participation in a co-op. The results have been mixed.

Here's a summary and my lessons learned for each:

- Alliances and joint ventures – I teamed with other professionals to pitch prospective clients or for RFP pitches. Projects ranged from consulting and studies to media production and on-call services. We had reasonable success winning contracts and the alliances definitely made us more competitive than if we had pitched ourselves alone. A big advantage was that this was a temporary arrangement, so I retained my independence.

One lesson learned was how this is a great way to test working relationships with other professionals connected with my field. It was a good practice to establish a simple letter of agreement covering key business relationship elements. The only pain points I experienced were some miscommunications during the proposal development and occasional creative differences during projects. Generally speaking, this has increasingly become my preferred way to scale my business over the years.

- Partnerships – I've formed a few partnership-based companies. These included corporations and LLCs. The purpose always was to combine our complementary skills, knowledge and contacts to provide a service or create products that would be challenging to produce on our own. Yes, a couple of these could have been set up by subcontracting certain functions to specialists but joint ownership was part of the plan.

    Positive aspects included shared responsibilities, being on a team, frequent interactions and idea exchanges, a focus on work activities we preferred, shared risk, increased output and some operational cost savings. The most frequent pain points were disagreements about the direction to take on projects, divergence regarding long-term goals, prioritizing expenditures, management of creative differences and issues involving communication that resulted in interpersonal friction that affected the businesses.

    Lessons learned? Think long and hard before forming partnerships to ensure that you and your partner(s) are on the same page regarding functional responsibilities, long-term goals, resolution of disagreements, decision-making processes and work-style compatibility. Many problems can be prevented by developing a good business plan. Also, take care in becoming partners with friends. While there are many advantages regarding trust and knowledge about each other, there are risks to those friendships if things go wrong with the venture. If your friendship is more important than the business, it might be better not to pursue a partnership together.

- Subcontracting – I've subcontracted a great many functions that I didn't have time for or that required special skills or equipment from professionals. My experience subcontracting has been great. Over time, you can identify a set of go-to pros for various needs and have confidence that the jobs will be done correctly, efficiently, on-time, on-budget and often exceeding your expectations.

  The main lesson learned here is to take good care of subcontractors and they'll take good care of you. This includes paying them well and on time, as well as respecting their ideas and judgement. It's also important to establish clear, detailed letters of agreements to keep things transparent. The only pain point here is when preferred subcontractors aren't available due to the timing, budget or location of projects. In those cases, you can ask them for referrals to pros they trust.

- Co-ops – I've interviewed with a co-op to consider participation. This was a closely-knit group of professionals with complementary skills that tended to pursue narrow target markets such as non-profits or small businesses. I learned that business models vary for co-ops. Some are loosely tied solo professionals, while others have formal expense and income sharing arrangements. The co-op I checked out just wasn't a good fit due to their narrow clientele emphasis and the partnership type structure. If you like the idea of being a part of a business group, a co-op may be worth considering.

19
Establishing Contracts and Agreements

Taking the time to establish contracts and agreements with clients is a necessary a pain point to endure. Even some associates of mine with many years of business experience have recounted instances when they started projects without proper contracts or agreements, sometimes with bad consequences.

There are many great resources written by attorneys and business advisors that spell out the elements of proper contracts and letters of agreement. I'm not qualified to offer legal advice on this subject, so my thoughts on this subject should only be taken as personal experience. Also, different professions and industries may require very different types of legal documents due to intellectual property, liability issues and other factors.

For the services I provide, I can tell you that five of the most important parts of these documents are: a clear description of the project, scope of work, schedule, costs and payment terms.

The description of the project ensures that my client and I agree on the nature of the project, general process to take place and the final deliverable(s). A detailed scope of work makes it clear what the client is paying me to do—and what's not included in the project—to prevent scope creep and misunderstandings about milestones or the work process. The need to include a mutually agreed upon schedule effectively manages expectations on steps and timing of deliverables. For my client's budgeting perspective and my business requirements, all hourly, flat fee, expense and other costs are spelled out. I never want a client to assume anything about the cost of doing business with me. Payment terms make it clear how, when and how much I'm paid for my services.

If there are changes to the project, client's management role, circumstances related to the project or unexpected events during work, my contract or agreement will protect both party's interests. Here's a sampling of situations that have occurred during projects that my contracts or agreements addressed effectively:

- The project grew in scale with more deliverables added, increasing costs and changing the schedule.

- Project managers changed during the work, so new ones needed to get up to speed on the project or desired alterations to aspects.

- Payments were late or amounts were incorrect, so the cost and terms were used as evidence for what was correct.

- The final deliverable date was moved up, compressing the schedule and increasing costs, or the date was extended which added downtime.

- Meetings and conference calls were added, increasing costs and expanding ongoing communication requirements.

- Access to subject matter experts and research requirements changed, causing delays and affecting expected processes.

- Aspects of the projects were moved to in-house staff, decreasing billable hours, changing the schedule and eliminating certain responsibilities.

- The project was cancelled part way through, so termination steps went into effect regarding payment for work completed and wrap up of activities.

All of these scenarios should be familiar to age 50-plus professionals. That's why it never fails to amaze me how many times such experienced businesspeople skip or delay establishing contracts or agreements before work commences. The excuses are that they've known the clients for years and trust them or the work really needed to begin right away and the paperwork could be dealt with in due time.

I don't consider contracts and agreements a reflection of my lack of trust in clients. I consider them tools to ensure that we're clear about our business relationship and that it's important for both of us to prevent any misunderstandings down the road.

20
Formulating Your Rates

One of the toughest pain points for age 50-plus professionals is establishing rates to charge clients. Our level of skills and knowledge—proven expertise—represents significant value to the clients we serve.

In some fields, such as consulting and product development, the link between value and cost isn't a major barrier. Performance and outcomes are what drive contracting decisions by clients. Sometimes this is a function of supply and demand, but also can be from a need that requires highly-specialized expertise or due to an unusual situation such as an emergency.

Most of us aren't in that position. We must take into account a variety of factors to set hourly or project rates. Factors include our overhead costs, our minimum acceptable rate, our professional credentials, how specialized our services are, our location and competitors' rates in our target client market. All of this these up to our value proposition, which usually is reflected by the range of our rates. I wish there were a magic formula for rates that took all this into account, but neither the data nor an algorithm is available to do that yet well.

Overhead costs are too often ignored when setting rates. Costs of doing business must be included in rates for a sustainable business model. Ongoing expenses may include phone, Internet, equipment, business service subscriptions, professional services, electricity and gas, auto expenses, rent (even for home offices), supplies, advertising, insurance, etc. This is a baseline amount before adding the cost of your time and resources.

Your minimum acceptable rate is the rock bottom hourly or project rate you'll accept, unless there's an extremely compelling reason to work at cost or a loss. Any fee below your overhead costs is working at a loss. I've had associates refer to the minimum acceptable rate as the "self-respect rate." They suggest that working for anything less is professionally insulting. It also means it isn't a professional approach.

Professional credentials range from years of experience in your field and level of expertise to degrees or certifications and client history. Let's say that your credentials elevate you to the top 10 percent of people in your field. Your rates probably should be in the highest range compared to others. This is a key component of your value to clients and must figure into your value proposition.

If you have highly specialized skills, knowledge or experience, that justifies higher rates just like your professional credentials do. A top expert in a specialty field likely is paid more than a generalist in that same field. Again, it's about the value you bring to your work and, therefore, to your clients.

It's unfair, but true, that your location can be a limiting or advantageous factor in setting your rates. For example, professional services rates on the two coasts of the U.S. traditionally have been higher than in the Midwest or South. Working remotely and living in a low-cost area of the country can be a competitive advantage. So, consider your overall costs of doing business in the context of your location and in your clients' locations when you formulate your rates.

As a highly experienced, 50-plus professional, I urge you to compete on the value you have to offer rather than just on rates. Competing mainly on rates, therefore being paid less and working too many hours a week, is a sure way to run yourself out of business. You cannot compete against free or minimum wage workers, wherever they're located.

Check the rates of comparably qualified contractors in your area and nationally who serve your target prospects. Calculate an acceptable range that's the basis for a profitable business model. Then, make your value proposition the core of your marketing efforts.

If price becomes an issue, first offer streamlined or fewer services. Remind prospects of the extra benefits of hiring you. Focus on what you can do for prospects based on their budgets, avoiding the temptation of discounting your services when negotiating contracts.

21
Packaging Your Services to Productize Them

Online contractor business platforms are driving a trend toward productization of a wide range of services. Essentially, this involves packaging and pricing an end product rather than charging for the hours to produce it. This is an emerging pain point that's affecting how many professionals can market their services. The downside is that it can devalue the experience, skill level and knowledge of age 50-plus professionals. Usually, it's a focus on price more than other factors.

Here's how the online model works. These platforms sign up contractors as on-call providers. Their services range from content marketing and graphic design to research and executive coaching. Buyers purchase packages of these services for one-time flat fees or monthly flat fee subscriptions. The platform handles the marketing and fee collection, paying the providers a flat fee no matter how much time it takes them to complete the projects.

To compete with these platforms and a growing marketplace that seems to prefer productization, some independent professionals are experimenting with the same model. For example, let's say you offer business plan development services. Traditionally, you prepare a proposal that's customized for the client. It includes a list of specific services tuned to their unique needs, time frames, your hourly rate and final deliverables.

The productization model changes this. A business plan "product" could be a flat fee for complete preparation of a 15-page plan. Interviews, research, writing and consulting would be built into this fee, determined by the average requirements of past projects like this. There still could be separate add-on packages for additional flat fees, such as an option for three hours of extra consulting or a 10-slide presentation deck for the plan.

The advantage for both parties is that this model is easy to understand due to being focused on the end product. Everyone knows the final cost. Services that always have been priced on an hourly basis now can be offered in a more transparent, but generic, way. In this model, services become commodities.

A disadvantage is that those end products representing a package of services are now marketed more on price than on quality, customization, experience of the providers and provider-client relationships. That's because the natural comparison to competitors will be package cost.

Service providers must play a game of averages with the hours and resources necessary to deliver the end products while keeping the final cost low enough to compete globally. This is a bit like converting a nuanced human-based service into a robotically or computer-based production model.

Will this turn into a race to complete projects as fast as possible to maximize profits versus a focus on quality, customer service and uniqueness of the product to support a brand? How do you convince a prospective client that your packaged service is worth more than the same end product from an online platform costing less? Will they value your experience, knowledge and skills or just focus on the product price?

I've experimented with productizing a couple of my communication services on a quiet and limited basis. The difference from a fully commoditized model is that I still established a contract with a clear scope of work and process for handling changes during the project. My projects tend to be more complex than just producing a simple widget, so some protections must be built in. I chose to price my time and resources on the average of similar past projects. I didn't base the package costs on the global market because those rates are completely unrealistic for my business overhead costs, required minimum wage and the professional value I offer my clients.

One project I secured ended up taking a bit more time than I built into the price. Another project actually required less time than anticipated. I'd say that everything worked out well overall. It's likely that I won't fully adopt this model because a big part of my brand revolves around highly customized services.

If you wish to productize services to fit this model, I suggest that you step into it incrementally. Some services can be packaged far more effectively than others. You don't want to become locked into a set pricing model at the sacrifice of the extra value you offer that makes your work expertly performed.

Take into account the competitive marketplace. However, remember that you've carved out a niche that separates your work from commodity type work.

22
Deciding Whether to Offer Discount Rates

It seems that everyone expects a deal. Depending upon the nature of your work and industry you serve, there's a good chance that you'll be asked to discount your rates. Also, you may be tempted to work for low rates to build your clientele or generate some cash flow. This can be an ongoing pain point in your business, especially for age 50-plus professionals requiring payment commensurate with our business credentials.

An associate of mine described a scenario that came from her experience soon after launching her business. As she pitched a growing number of prospects for her services, many of them said they were interested but her fees were far higher than what they saw on online job platforms. They said that those other consultants were willing to take on initial projects at very cheap rates. Her prospects didn't consider lowest cost providers much of a risk due to their cheap rates.

My associate said that she was tempted to match those deals or offer a discount to at least compete with them. She thought about her extensive experience and high-value services and then decided not to play the discount game. She could offer verified expertise, a far more engaged relationship, high confidence that her work will exceed clients' expectations and competitive rates compared to professionals with her experience.

She also noted that greatly discounting her rates could risk setting a precedent that would put pressure on her to lower her rates again for these and future clients. We agreed that highly experienced talent's value proposition is just that… value. High value costs more than low value.

The three most common scenarios regarding discounting our fees are: (1) Promises of future work if your rates are cut for the first project, (2) promises of "great exposure" in exchange for discounted rates and (3) requests for pro bono (donated) services.

Although promises for future work if an initial project rate is discounted may be well intentioned, this is a bad bet the vast majority of the time. I've fallen for this several times on projects I was particularly interested in working on or with clients I thought had a lot of potential as long-term relationships. The future work never, I repeat never, came about. Most often, this is a ruse to pay as little as possible to get high-value work.

The other risk with this is that they may very well request continuation of your discounts on future projects since you already set the precedent of cheapening your services to accommodate their "needs." If they could afford your full rates later, they can afford them at the start. I suggest that you'd be better off pitching some extra services you provide as part of your services to clients instead of offering discounts.

Promises of "great exposure" if you discount rates for work is code for "we don't want to pay you" or "we have no money." Your work has value for clients. One way or another, your work makes them money or saves them money. If they are paid for that, you should be as well. Working for free is not a sustainable business model.

That said, there are a few cases when investing your services with a client might make sense. For example, a client might offer to promote your name or company to their audience. If their audience size or target audience fits your marketing plan, then a test may be worth it. Trading services (bartering) can work in cases when it's very likely to be equally mutually beneficial.

Startups tend to be the most frequent adopters of the exposure for work scheme. In those cases, consider asking for equity in exchange for a defined period of non-paid or discounted services. Another option is to establish an agreement for deferred payment, with a set number of months in the future when they have revenue. My best advice is to only enter into these arrangements strategically, not just on hopes and promises, and negotiate the best deal you can.

Pro bono work makes sense when you want to support a non-profit with your time and expertise rather than a monetary donation. I've found occasional pro bono work very rewarding as a way to give back to my community. Of course, there's usually some type of recognition for this which can increase your visibility but that really isn't the point. Be aware that once the word gets out that you've offered pro bono services to organizations, you may be contacted with requests from others quite often. Except in rare circumstances, I limit myself to one pro bono project or maybe two projects per year.

23
Testing Niche Services to Penetrate a Market

An effective way to establish a market position and build your business is to experiment with your marketing efforts by focusing on niches. This means you pitch certain skills and services to specific target markets. It's in contrast to marketing as a generalist in your field or reaching out to a wide variety of potential clients. Too often, overly expansive marketing efforts are the default for age 50-plus professionals and a pain point due to its inefficiency.

I'm not saying that you should concentrate your long-term efforts on marketing only one skill or going after a very narrow group of clients. I'm advocating for an overall marketing strategy that includes experimentation with niches to test opportunities. These might be niches ignored by your competition or ones that you can dominate due to a highly customized approach.

Ultimately, you want to aim to build visible and profitable positions within several niches. This would be a component of your marketing plan while still offering a variety of services to a reasonably broad market to ensure diversification.

Let's say that you're a programmer who develops Web sites. You can develop just about any type of site for any type of client using the most popular programming languages. That's just like thousands of other developers around the world. You can market your services to everyone you can reach, but that isn't very efficient. It's like randomly sending out a boilerplate email to 1,000 companies across the country and hoping for a one percent response rate.

What if you take a niche approach instead? First, you consider the types of Web sites you prefer building, the knowledge you have about particular industries, your credibility with a category of businesses and other characteristics that set you apart from other programmers. Then, you focus your marketing efforts on one or two niches associated with the following:

- A specific industry or audience with which you have a connection.
- Prospects in need of programming in a specific language or on a special platform.
- Sites designed for a specific purpose, such as sales, education, news or outreach.
- The type of site content, such as ones that are media-rich, interactive or multi-language.
- Site re-designs or upgrades.
- Target prospects in a single location, such as locally, regionally or in a particular country.
- Sites that feature a particular design style.

Another highly relevant niche for some 50-plus professionals is to focus on our own demographic. Find ways to target other age 50-plus clients. There's a good chance that they operate their own businesses or are in the C-suite of larger companies.

A slightly different entry point is to look for products and services catering to our demographic and, then, market to those companies based on your services tailored to their needs and related to serving people our age. After all, who knows the needs of age 50-plus clients and customers better than someone our age? This idea could be developed many ways as our specialty.

If one niche doesn't work out, you move on to others. The goal is to experiment to find niches—pain points that you can address in selected markets—that yield the number and type of clients you want to have for the projects you want to do. These are called "verticals" as you're building depth in defined areas. At the same time, you remain open to general work that comes your way. That allows you to remain diversified and maintain steady revenues to be able to experiment with new niches.

I warn associates about becoming overly dependent on single niches. It's like only knowing how to use one software tool. If something dramatically changes in the customer's market and it's no longer the tool in-demand, you suddenly could be left with no clients. Niches typically come and go, so the hunt for new ones should be unending.

It's also a good idea to look for niches outside your comfort zone. Look beyond your obvious client market based on your experience or connections. This allows you to explore new types of opportunities and pushes you to build on your skills and knowledge. What are your transferable skills? Which categories of new clients might need those skills and value the perspective you offer when considering your previous work? How can you re-frame your skills and knowledge to appeal to specific new audiences?

I encourage you to experiment with skill and market niches. Depth and diversification are the foundation of a sustainable and profitable contracting business.

24
Defending Against Income Volatility

Being an independent professional means that you accept the risk of income volatility. You have good months and tough ones; sometimes good years and not so good ones. Diversification with multiple income streams can be the key to enhance revenue stability for your business.

The main reasons to establish multiple income streams are to stabilize your revenue and generate passive income. There are great benefits of pursuing one or both of these efforts to prevent pain points of income gaps.

Diversifying your income generating activities involves developing multiple income sources in connection with your core work activities that are paid as hourly or project fees. Passive income is revenue that's not as dependent on or completely independent of the hours you work. Think consulting hours versus online fees for access to a training program you developed based your area of work. This passive income fulfills the common definition of entrepreneurship, which involves building a business bigger than yourself or your hours worked.

How do you accomplish this? Any or all of the following activities can diversify your businesses:

- Adding services – If you're a specialized professional, you may wish to diversify your services by looking for elements of your work that can be transferable to other categories of services or to different target clients. Continuing education may be a route to offering new skills. Listen to clients and study your industry to identify pain points that you could address and for which you could develop new services as solutions. I started my business offering only one service, but over time that grew to well over a dozen types of services. This has been the case for most of my associates. Clients asked them for help in new areas, opportunities arose to apply skills to different types of projects and the range of projects that interested them changed.

- Consulting – If you provide services, look for ways to repurpose your knowledge and skills in the form of consulting. I was drawn into consulting by clients who used my project services and wanted me to advise them on areas of planning, strategy development and project management. I have numerous associates who found that guiding others to perform work activities better was more challenging and rewarding than offering those services directly. In other words, they began helping clients do the work rather than doing the work for them.

- Training – Consider developing live or recorded training services, built on your experience and knowledge, such as workshops or courses. If you create an online or downloadable training program, it can generate passive income from enrollments due to auto-delivery of the program. I've offered a variety of live training services leveraging specific skills I have. Some of my associates teach part-time at local colleges as well as offer workshops through professional organizations and at conferences. Also, some solo entrepreneurs have such success with their training packages or presentations that they "franchised" them by licensing others to deliver that training. This is a way to build a business far larger than your solo enterprise.

- Writing – Find opportunities for paid writing related to your expertise, such as articles, columns, guest blogging and co-authoring. If you write a book about your work experience, you can generate passive income from sales. For several years, I was a business journalist writing for many publications as I provided technical writing services to clients. Quite a few of my associates have written books for the income and because they're great marketing tools for their businesses.

- Speaking – If you're comfortable speaking to groups, you can earn significant income from keynotes at clients' internal meetings and at conferences. Recordings of speeches and presentations can generate passive income online through downloads or as part of training packages. Speaking has raised the visibility of many of my associates in addition to revenue from those engagements. The higher visibility increased offers for contracts for their services and positioned them for opportunities to move their businesses in new directions. Paid speaking is a way to significantly increase your earnings per hour. That can mean that you have the choice to reduce your hours spent on your typical client services.

- Video blogs and podcasts – Your knowledge and industry perspective have value. Video blogs and podcasts are popular ways to monetize this value through subscriptions. Having a large network of contacts is a big advantage, as you can start with or market to a significant audience. Some of my associates have had such great success with podcasts that they've chosen to cut back on their other work. Plus, the exposure from broadcasting content resulted in many other business opportunities. Monetized (e.g., paid per view or subscription) video blogs and podcasts are great examples of building passive income not dependent on your hours worked.

- Products – Depending upon the work you do and industry, you might have ideas for physical products you could develop and sell.

I've known management consultants who have created business games and creative tools that teach collaboration, inclusion, creativity and other skills. For example, a real estate expert I know created software for professionals in his industry. Sales of products create passive income and help build a business that's not dependent on selling your hours.

- Equity in clients' businesses – If you work with startups or small businesses that have limited funds to pay you for your services, you could discuss payment by earning equity in their businesses. Your eventual payment might result from dividends, a buy-out by the founders or a cash-out if the clients' companies are sold or go public with their stock. Be sure to perform your due diligence before entering into arrangements like this. You might want to consult an attorney or business advisor to ensure that the contracts protect your rights and secure the right deals.

25
Offering Alternatives to Payment for Cash-Strapped Clients

I think it would be safe to say the majority of age 50-plus professionals operate by an inflexible rule: "No pay, no play." In other words, prospective clients who don't have the funds to pay for services should wait until they do before asking for professional services. That may be a pain point because, in some cases, it can be short-sighted.

If your cash-flow situation requires that you focus your time and effort only on paying clients, that's the right choice. You've got to pay the bills and be paid yourself. However, it might be a good idea to be open to alternative compensation when you have enough paying clients to cover overhead and some compensation. Why? Because there are arrangements that may pay off in other ways or in greater amounts in the long-run.

For example, "other ways" might include loyalty-based relationships, such as a contractual commitment to work with you at a certain point in their growth. The "greater amounts" I mentioned could be your accumulated fees, equity in the client's business or monetary bonuses in some form. This may be an especially attractive option for age 50-plus professionals who have the business experience to make sound judgements in these cases.

Here's an example from my experience. I was introduced to a cash-strapped prospective client via a referral from an associate. Their team was authentic, passionate and had great products. I quickly learned that they needed assistance from someone with my services and experience. We ended up establishing a contract with my services being paid in company stock.

Without getting into the details, it worked out to be a fair arrangement all around. I'll benefit from their success, part of which should result from my services. So, when the company is sold or taken public or when dividends are paid, the value of my investment in them likely will increase significantly. The income potential may be far higher than if I just received payment for hours worked. I did specify a limit to the amount of work I would provide over time, as I couldn't afford to over-commit to this type of speculative relationship.

In addition to negotiating attractive equity payment agreements, you might consider deferred payment, contracts for future work, barter deals, commission-based contracts or other creative alternatives to direct payment. Sometimes contracts like these are very simple and relatively low risk. If you sense elevated risk or the dollar amounts could be quite high, it might be best to consult a business lawyer for guidance and to review the contracts. Be aware that any of these alternative payment arrangements could have tax and regulatory implications that must be researched prior to commencement of the deals.

Deferred payment might involve logging your hours over the defined period so that the full amount can be paid at a set date. You might charge a higher rate due to the delay in payment or set up a mutually agreed upon bonus to be added as compensation.

A contract for future work is just that. The client agrees to hire you for a certain number of hours each month in the future or maybe put you on retainer starting when a certain revenue level is reached. Your rate may reflect the value of this delayed payment to the client.

Barter deals work when your client has products or services you need that offer an equitable amount of value as that of your services. Be aware that there are tax implications with bartering.

Commission-based contracts could involve you earning a percentage of the client's new business somehow tied to your work. Depending upon the nature of the business, you might need to set up a tracking system for this.

There are other creative alternatives being used by independent professionals. For example, I have associates who accept payment in cryptocurrencies.

Besides the equity arrangement with one company, I've employed deferred payment, future work and commission-based options a handful of times. There have been a few times when I wasn't paid the full amounts due for my work and only a couple arrangements have completely failed to pay. I typically have one or two of these alternative compensation arrangements active most years as "investments" to earn a larger return than just from my hourly or project rates. Most often, this involves work with a promising startup.

My warning about any alternative payment arrangement is that there are real risks of not getting paid or compensated for your work. Many things can go right and wrong, with the majority being out of your control. Only commit to an alternative arrangement after appropriate research, expert guidance and solid agreements or contracts. Use knowledge from your years of business experience to evaluate these opportunities as a consultant or investor would.

26
Providing On-Call Services

There are significant benefits to offering on-call services to clients, as well as some challenges. A big plus is having a steady stream of projects offered to you over long periods with clients you come to know very well. The pain points include the following: assignments can occur at inconvenient times, occasionally are high-pressure and may require a fair amount of resourcefulness due to the level of independence you're given. All in all, on-call services can be a great fit for age 50-plus professionals due to the relationship and communication aspects deep business experience supports.

An on-call relationship may be associated with an umbrella contract for your services over a given period for a set hourly rate. Frequently, on-call arrangements are just initiated as an understanding between you and a manager at a company. You're positioned as a client's go-to, first-choice service provider. This is an ongoing relationship with your rates potentially varying according to the services provided or nature of the projects.

I've been fortunate to have had numerous on-call service relationships in my career. Many spanned several years while a couple thrived for 12 years or more. Most of these clients initially engaged me for only one or two of my services. Over time, additional services were requested, with some I learned on-the-job or via self-directed training. There were periods of full-time work as well as some gaps, but they involved a pretty regular stream of small to large projects every month or year.

Additionally, I was hired a few times as what's called a sole-source on-call contractor. This was a fast-track hiring process for single, large projects that required significant subject knowledge and experience with an organization.

How do you address the pain point of finding and establishing on-call arrangements? Government on-call contracts typically are offered by request for proposals (RFPs) or by sole-source contracts that bypass standard RFP procedures. Agencies also might have on-call contracting opportunities offered only to a pre-arranged pool of contractors, often for projects with total costs under a set threshold. These tend to be awarded to contractors with whom the staff previously worked, by referrals or through visibility among staff members via outreach, conferences or other connections.

Private sector businesses occasionally advertise such arrangements but more often than not I've found that they evolve from a successful single project that turns into a series of assignments. The seems to hold true with non-profit entities, when one project leads to many. Again, these arrangements frequently arise via referrals and some type of previous contact with managers and employees. Because on-call contracting opportunities may not be formal arrangements or not advertised, your search for them must be ongoing, through networking and by building relationships.

What contractor performance tends to lead to on-call arrangements? The keys to successful long-term, on-call arrangements are the same as for building any solid portfolio of clients. Here are some traits that my clients have said they look for:

- Solid experience and proven skills delivered on-time and on-budget, with competitive rates.

- Desire to learn about the client's business, including their industry, culture, challenges, processes and contracting procedures.

- Businesslike attitude and professional level business practices.

- Effective communication and collaboration skills.

- Clear and professional letters of agreement and project contracts.

- Willingness to drop everything at times for urgent projects. This can mean working some evenings and weekends, as necessary.

- Ability to perform with minimal supervision and direction.

- Resourcefulness and project management skills to get the job done despite challenges.

- Quality control to ensure work is done correctly the first time.

- Willingness to take the initiative to enhance skills or learn new ones based on client requests.

- Desire to provide exceptional service and go the extra mile to make clients look good and help their enterprises succeed.

27
Managing Client Relationship Challenges

An advantage of having worked a long time is that you've likely acquired considerable knowledge about what goes on behind the scenes at companies. You are well aware of operational pain points. It's likely you've coped with poor internal communication, turf battles, egos, less than qualified colleagues, bad leaders, company downturns, project disasters, failed change management initiatives, budget battles, team conflicts and maybe even ageism within an organization's culture.

Intra-organizational pain points don't go away when working with organizations as an outside contractor. Being the outsider can add complexity to working with clients when such issues infiltrate projects. Based on stories from my associates and my own experience, here are some common situations we've encountered as contractors in which our age or experience level were factors, along with example solutions:

- Working with much younger project leads and experiencing indications that ageism is a problem – Keep the focus on communications about the project, your strategies and solutions, and indirectly the value you are providing. Avoid situations that set up comparisons of professional experience, discussions about the "ways things have always been done," "time tested methods," and advice or decisions that question or test the manager's authority. You are an expert or you wouldn't have been hired. So, use appropriate diplomacy to avoid age-related issues and, if any arise, quickly diffuse them by pivoting to the project and the shared goal of success with it.

- Being tempted to provide unsolicited feedback on the project or project management – Maintain your attention on the scope of work in your contract. If a situation arises with a project that calls for advice on the periphery or outside the project (but on factors that could affect it), it's often best to frame that feedback as questions rather than statements or direct suggestions. Look for opportunities to bring up your insights within the context of problem-solving conversations or message exchanges.

- Asking questions as issues occur or information gaps surface – Just because you have extensive experience in your field doesn't mean that you won't have questions for clients as projects proceed. It's likely that you can work independently and use research as your first action when questions arise. That said, thoughtful and clearly asked questions can help build trust and more collaborative relationships. Our questions don't threaten clients' perceptions of our expertise. This is part of our role.

- Adjusting to a client's management and communications culture – Listen, listen, listen. Many companies, especially startups, have their own cultural quirks and unique styles. Your job is to adapt to those characteristics rather than resist or question them. The exception is when you've been hired for change management or other functions associated with operational improvement.

- Building trust that you understand the client, their business and current trends – It's critical to do your homework about prospective clients before you're hired. You should understand far more than just what the project description includes. Your proposal, interview and ongoing communication should provide opportunities to convey your knowledge about the client, their business and current trends. If you're not up to speed on everything, except inside information related to the project, then you probably won't get the contract or don't deserve it. You're too experienced to enter relationships unprepared.

- Providing emergency services – Clients who hire experienced professionals at crunch-times usually have both realistic and unrealistic expectations. A relationship involving saving the project or company from a disaster is a great opportunity to use your expertise, as long as you're clear about what's possible to accomplish. If you don't address unrealistic expectations early, you could be setting yourself up for failure. Propose your plan and execute it efficiently, with extensive communication along the way. Also, decide if you want to set the precedent of being "the emergency expert." I've served that role with several clients and, despite the pressure and wild schedules for work, it built some long-term, profitable relationships.

- Reacting to circumstances when things go wrong with projects – You must be the calm and reassuring one in the room. Based on your experience addressing challenges in your work, you should be well-prepared to methodically guide clients through tough situations to turn things around.

Experience provides you with perspective, judgement, empathy, respect and a track record of problem-solving. That positions you well for effectively managing most challenges with client relationships. Chances are that surprises along the way won't shock you and you'll take them in stride. You can be the one to reassure clients that you, as part of their team, can help them overcome any challenges that present themselves.

28
Controlling Client Interaction Time on Projects

Meetings, collaborations and check-ins can be huge schedule busters and budget pain points, especially for highly experience professionals. This is not to say that client communication is unimportant. On the contrary, it's critical. But it's common for these communications to quickly exceed time estimates in proposals and decrease hours available to perform the core work of the contract.

This is a challenge for professionals of any age. However, I've been asked to participate in more conference calls and meetings ever since I was deemed "senior level" in my profession. I also receive far more calls from project managers during contract work, often to provide consulting on business on the edges or outside the contracts' scopes of work.

With conference calls and meetings, I'm asked to listen in for my take on what's happening internally with projects or to provide my outsider's perspective. Also, project managers tend to make extra efforts to keep me up to date on aspects of the projects. Frequently, they ask for my thoughts on planning, trends related to the projects or input on other activities.

I'm honored to be integrated with project teams and considered a valuable contributor. However, the time spent on those interactions often exceeds the amount of time estimated by clients when we're specifying line items of hours per task or activity in the scope of work. To prepare for this, I build in additional time along with my justification, if necessary.

Many of my age 50-plus associates indicate they've experienced the same phenomenon as they achieved senior level credentials. Several pointed out that this may depend on how narrow the professional's specialty is and, to a certain degree, the industry they work in.

My associates who provide services such as accounting, programming, engineering and some areas of consulting say that client interactions exceed estimates only occasionally, maybe due to the highly focused nature of their projects. Those who provide design, management consulting, communications, project management and similar services seem to experience far higher demands for unanticipated client interactions. Honestly, I'm not sure if there's enough evidence to make any conclusions about specialties, industries and client interaction trends.

One way to help control scope creep regarding client interactions is by addressing this issue specifically at the contract development stage. That's when an estimate for hours or flat fees for this line item is made. I ask about the number of meetings and conference calls planned, but also a guess about the number of additional ones typical for projects like this one. I also try to nail down the frequency and duration of status or check-in calls, collaboration calls, and "other" discussions to expect.

In the media production industry, the unknowns about projects fall into a what's commonly called a contingency budget. All contract professionals should consider adding such a line item or basing estimated costs for client communication, meetings and other interactions on worst case scenarios. At a minimum, consider including a note in agreements about how this issue will be handled. I state that if interaction hours look like they're trending above estimates, a change order for our contract may be required. This would be to ensure that budgets for other aspects of the project aren't negatively affected.

Once a project is underway, it's a good idea to bring up this issue with the project manager as soon as there's evidence that excessive interactions could affect the budget. We usually settle on the highest priority type meetings, conference calls and other calls. Also, we identify lower priority interactions to reduce or eliminate to avoid additional expenses.

These two approaches work most of the time. For long-term clients, I tend to be far more flexible about such interactions. There have been plenty of times I haven't charged for calls on topics at the periphery of the scopes of work or completely outside them. I consider these investments in our relationships. For single project clients, especially with inflexible contract budgets, I'm more proactive in managing interaction time.

I think we must find the right balance for this pain point depending on the client, the nature of the project and contract.

29
Pitching Ideas to Clients

When you're hired for your extensive experience developing "fresh ideas" and your "outside perspective," you tend to have certain expectations on how receptive clients will be to your thinking. They should welcome your brilliant ideas, right? Well, it depends and too often becomes a pain point.

I've pitched countless approaches and solutions to clients over the years. Pitches have been delivered in writing, verbally and via multimedia presentations. I built sound business cases for the ideas I proposed and the majority of my ideas were well-received.

However, when I wanted to push comfort zones with unconventional or highly creative ideas, I felt far more pressure to craft pitches that addressed the expected resistance. There was risk associated with pitching big ideas so that affected the pitch development process itself.

All of your professional experience in your field doesn't necessarily equip you to pitch big and maybe even disruptive level ideas as an outsider of an organization. We all know that doing that as an employee can risk your job, especially if you're given a go-ahead and the effort fails. Most businesspeople are conditioned to play it safe even when they know such an approach often leads to mediocrity and increased risk from competition.

Pitching what are sometimes big, business-changing ideas and approaches has been a critical element of my work. When I develop pitches like these, I initially focus on my audience and what their pain points are. I need to have a picture of how well they understand the pain point, what their concerns or fears are, what's at stake, what types of solutions they're accustomed to embracing and how the pain points are connected to other issues or functions of their business.

Additionally, I try to understand any other background information that offers context for their pain points. This helps direct me toward the right content for my idea or approach but also how to present my pitch.

I try to hook my client's attention right from the start within the framework of a story. Their problem is the conflict that needs to be resolved. This means we're talking about touching emotions and setting the stage for an evidence-based argument supporting a set of actions to take. You do this because you need their attention and to get them to listen.

There are occasions when the only choice is to build a story around the risk or negative consequences of not effectively addressing the problem. My preferred angle is to focus on the benefits of using my proposed ideas or approaches—all the emphasis is on positives.

For example, the opening of your pitch can be to entice a client to imagine a scenario in which their problem is resolved. Guide them to visualize your big idea or approach being successful and the impact of that on their operations, marketing or sales, industry position, or whatever area of their business would be affected most by the problem being eliminated. Then, move on to how this can be accomplished by a set of well thought-out, evidence-based steps.

Here are a few more tips on pitching ideas and approaches:

- Focus on the compelling aspects of the idea itself, not just on general benefits such as the monetary potential or "change the world" effect. What's the emotional, inspirational, memorable and meaningful core of this idea that will drive benefits and, ultimately, success?

- Use some familiar terms, examples and concepts in the description of your idea or approach so it doesn't sound completely foreign to the audience. Sometimes a good option is to compare aspects of your idea to one of their recent efforts that was highly successful.

- Frame and define the problem by identifying the underlying cause and build a logical argument and flexible steps to solve it.

- Support your commitment to establishing or maintaining the organization's superior market position, staying ahead of disruptive competition and supporting an innovation-centered culture.

- When defining the problem to be addressed, explain why it matters, what it means to solve it and what's needed to solve it efficiently and effectively.

30
Working Remotely With Clients

It seems that nearly every type of service can be provided at least partly on a remote basis. Of course, certain elements of consulting, training, coaching, project management, technical services, product design work, etc. must be conducted on-site due to the required facilities or level of interaction necessary. However, age 50-plus professionals have seen the transition from a high percentage of contract work being conducted on-site to the current trend towards remote, on-demand and outsourced contract services.

I've worked remotely with clients for nearly all of my career. Sometimes it seemed odd to me that I hadn't met in person the majority of my clients across the U.S. and abroad. With increasing use of conference calls, video calls, online collaboration platforms, emails and text messaging, shared cloud storage of files, and other communication and collaboration tools, it is easier than ever to work remotely.

Working remotely isn't without its pain points, though. Here are some challenges I've experienced and solutions that have helped me prevent or address issues:

- Team inclusiveness – Physical proximity makes teamwork easier, due to the chance for spontaneous conversations, the immediacy of sharing products or materials, opportunities for ad hoc meetings, and other aspects. When you're not present with your team, you just don't have the same level of participation as other team members. This can lead to not being up to date on some developments, decisions, issues and nuances about the progress of projects. Sometimes these things don't come up during calls or other communications.

The best solution I've found is to regularly communicate one-on-one with multiple team members. Ask plenty of questions, including ones such as, "Is there anything else I should know about regarding the team or this project?" Typical status reports or exchanges tend not to cover what's going on behind the scenes, so less structured conversations work better.

- Feedback about projects – It can be common to feel like you're working blindly at times as the remote worker. You might submit a report, parts of the project or other deliverables and receive inadequate feedback or even silence. This really depends on how responsive the client's project managers or teams are during the life cycle of the projects. Another factor is how accustomed they are to working with remote professionals.

The only solution I've found to resolve this is to directly ask for feedback, sometimes on a very specific level. For example, instead of just asking, "What do you think about this deliverable?" I might ask, "Have I missed anything at this stage?" and "Do you have suggestions to improve this deliverable?" If these types of questions don't elicit the responses I need, I might identify very specific elements of the work and ask for notes or line item level comments. When all else fails, I call clients to review a document together or analyze the project step-by-step.

- Information security – Some projects involve proprietary content or sensitive information covered by non-disclosure agreements. These warrant security concerns. Security can be a major issue with companies and some government agencies when working with contractors remotely. I've had projects in which written materials and messages couldn't be exchanged by email or an unsecured platform. I had to provide password protected or encrypted storage of files on my computers and backup systems.

When such issues arose, I explained what I could and couldn't provide for information security. My clients always were helpful in providing direction on what I needed to do. So, the solution was to be honest about my capabilities.

- Expendability – Remote contractors are far easier to terminate than employees. Sometimes projects just evaporate and so the need for the contractor. Budgets are cut, project managers and teams are reassigned, projects are determined unnecessary, and clients' needs change. This is a fact of life for those of us operating on a remote basis.

  If you maintain effective communication with your clients, there's a better chance that you'll be informed early or recognize hints about projects ending early. Unfortunately, there's no solution to being expendable. One thing you can do is to try to remain aware of other project opportunities with the client to position yourself in a way that you can pivot to another project if the current one ends. If your project is terminated, make a respectful and professional exit. Since you earned one project with that client, you want to remain in good standing for one in the future.

31
Practicing the Right Level of Customer Service

Age 50-plus professionals tend to create a pain point around customer service. It's not that we don't provide outstanding customer service. Chances are that our experience has taught us that providing top notch services, being very responsive in work and communications, completing projects on time and on budget, and following through on promises is the way to build lasting and profitable relationships.

The problem is when we cross the line by providing such an extraordinary level customer service that we're giving too much away and setting an unsustainable precedent. We each must have a flexible limit for what we do to exceed our clients' expectations without the need to charge additional fees. This can occur from our desire to show the exceptional amount of effort and how we invest in our business relationships.

Often, additional services are informally requested by clients. In these cases, you must determine if it's appropriate to provide the services or if this is an indication of project scope creep. You must decide whether the new task should be a legitimate line item added to the scope of work.

Unless I want to absorb the cost of these services as a worthwhile investment in the relationships, I discuss the work changes with my clients in a positive manner. In their defense, many times clients forget that we're contractors and accidentally treat us like employees without such defined contractual boundaries for our work.

I'm all for doing small favors for clients whether those activities are related to the project for which I've been hired or even a bit outside the project. It builds plenty of goodwill. But when it feels like the client is intentionally or unintentionally taking advantage of my generosity, I make it clear in advance that there will be extra costs for performing the additional activities. Again, cases of obvious scope creep must be controlled by discussing the change order to the contract when the services are requested.

Have I been taken advantage of on occasion? Yes. After completing projects, I've regretted leaving legitimately earned money on the table. However, I probably felt worse about not sticking to the scope of work in the contract. Did doing that extra work at no charge result in more projects from those clients? Sometimes it did, which I appreciated. However, it's usually best to avoid crossing the line beyond strategic generosity or you'll start failing to value your services.

In addition to offering a high level of customer service to clients on projects, I often provide a type of customer service that has successfully grown profitable ongoing relationships. When I run across an article that may be of interest to a client, I'll forward that with a brief note explaining why I thought it was relevant. This note might read something like, "I thought of you and your work involving [fill in the topic] when I read this article. I look forward to working with you on another project soon." Sometimes I'll connect my services to the article by saying, "This article is about [fill in the topic] and I thought you'd find it informative. I may not have mentioned that I also provide [fill in the type of service at least somewhat related to the article] in addition to how I contributed to our previous collaboration."

Outstanding customer service gives you the opportunity to prompt clients to remember that you did a great job on a project. They'll recall that it was nice to work with you as well as how you went above and beyond along the way. You want to be that memorable contractor who remains on the client's radar for future work.

What is the right level of customer service for you? Only you can decide. It's a balancing act sometimes. Much of the decision about limits revolves around how well a client treats you, as relationships are a two-way street. If you're treated very nicely by a client, it feels natural to treat them well.

Good clients understand that your time and expertise costs them money. Just be careful not to be taken advantage of or sacrifice earned income by being the overly generous person you are.

32
Surviving Work Overload Periods

Too much work? That's a problem we all say we want to have. A case might be when multiple prospects notify you that you've been awarded contracts or several projects come your way unexpectedly due to associates' referrals. That's all when you may have a full plate of work already. So, yes there are times when work comes in big waves and cause a too-good-to-be-true pain point.

Chances are that your years of experience, qualifications or large number of existing relationships from years in your field results in clients wanting to hire you. They don't want the work to be subcontracted or get a referral from you. I don't know if this is more common with highly experienced professionals than with others. However, I've heard from my clients that proven skills and trust are big factors in their desire to contract with professionals who have many years of work under their belts.

An impossible pain point to ignore is that you only have so many hours in the day—and sometimes nights and weekends—to juggle multiple projects. That is, while maintaining your concentration and energy to produce work up to your standards. There are many times when projects require full-time attention to meet deadlines, as well.

Whenever this has happened to me it's been a challenging situation. I take my contracts very seriously, not just as business agreements but as personal, professional commitments to my clients. When we agree to schedules, they know I'll make sure the work will be done to high standards and on time. Professional reliability is the cornerstone of a successful business.

One of our worst fears as independent professionals is to say no to desirable projects or contracts because our schedules are full. We want to be the go-to resources for clients. Plus, what could be the short and long-term consequences of turning down these opportunities?

In many cases, you must respond quickly so you should be prepared with an approach. The first thing I do is ask about the schedule for the project and if it's flexible. I explain that I've got a full slate of projects and will need to determine whether I can take on more work while providing the level of service I'm committed to. If their schedule is flexible and it fits well with my current projects, then it's an easy decision to say yes. If their timeline is problematic, I ask if I can call back later that day or the next day so I can figure out if I can adjust my other projects. I don't think anyone has ever told me I couldn't do that. Although, it hasn't been unusual for them to reiterate the urgency of my decision at the end of the call.

Let's say I really want to accept this new project but by taking it on I know I can't fulfill other work commitments for my current clients. In this case, I'll check my existing project schedules and milestones to see if I can delay any steps. If a minor change would result in adequate time for me to slip in the new work, I'll contact the current client(s) and ask if it would be okay to make schedule changes.

I'm always up front with clients. I'll be honest in saying that the reason for my request is that an urgent project has come up with another client. I assure them that their project is still a top priority and it'll be completed on time as promised. If they aren't comfortable with a change, I'll stand by my commitment to them. However, I wouldn't have asked them for a schedule change if I didn't think an adjustment could be made. I've almost always been granted the requested change.

My best advice regarding this unusual pain point is to be loyal to existing clients. Never allow yourself to become overloaded to the degree that schedules or quality of your work will suffer. If it turns out that you must decline a project, explain the situation to the prospect. They'll respect your professionalism. After all, they could be on the other end of a situation like this with you in the future and expect you to respond with the same integrity.

BUSINESS SUSTAINABILITY AND GROWTH PAIN POINTS

33
Seeking the Right Clients

I've heard many associates repeat the mantra, "Any paying client is the right client." That may be the case for many startups, but as highly experienced talent we often can launch from a different starting point with our businesses.

We already have connections with the types of prospective clients we want to work with. This affords us the opportunity to target a defined group of prospects in marketing efforts to minimize the pain point of prospecting for "just any" business, including clients we really don't prefer.

Consider focusing on the right or ideal prospective clients first. Think about how you'd describe your ideal clients or customers. Factors could include the size of the business, the industry or sector they're in, the types of products or services they sell, your past relationship with staff members, the organization's culture, the size of budgets they have for your services, or even their location (e.g., local businesses offering face-to-face contact). Chances are that you can make a list of these prospects from your work history, including the names of initial contacts in some organizations.

The right clients also can be the best ones to target strategically. By this I mean identifying certain prospects that, if successfully engaged for projects, can open doors in related areas.

For example, an associate who is an author, consultant and speaker has used strategic prospect marketing to reach his ideal prospects—to get on their radar and have credibility with them. He spoke at relatively small conferences for their low compensation to build his credentials to speak at larger industry events. His strategy was to get in front of audiences who included executives at companies he wanted to target for specialized speaking events and consulting. Although his keynotes became a significant revenue source, his paid workshop and training oriented speaking at companies and non-profits cleared the way for consulting contracts. He felt that these audiences would be the best way to achieve his mission of moving an industry in a better direction when it came to certain business practices.

Other associates have cleverly marketed their deep experience working in industries to get highly targeted consulting engagements. Specifically, they focused on engaging with multinational companies to position themselves for international consulting, training or speaking opportunities. For some associates, this was to establish a way for their work to support their love of travel or interest in connecting with the global economy.

With some research, they identified companies that had major offices in the countries they wanted to visit. A strategy to facilitate this was to start by working with these companies' local or regional offices. This way, they had the right contacts to approach and could establish credibility with those organizations. It was an easy transition to then pitch their services internationally to these clients.

You always can expand your marketing efforts to additional prospects later, even some who are in the margins of the types you want to work with. This is on top of seizing opportunities to pitch prospects who come to your attention or approach you from referrals, industry visibility or through other means.

At least in the early stages of your business development, why not choose the people and organizations with whom you work? That's one of the big advantages of being in business for yourself. This is especially important to many of us at age 50-plus because we want to minimize the need to pay our dues like we did earlier in our careers. Our goal is to only work with clients who align with our mission and business goals.

34
Devising Ways to Make the Most of Referrals and Inside Tracks

An unfortunate pain point for many age 50-plus professionals is that they often underestimate the value of their industry contact networks. Also, they may not understand how to leverage those contacts to accelerate business growth.

Contact networks are assets that take a long time to build. They're your trusted relationships formed through collaboration, work, school, associations, conferences and other business connections. Your contacts are the right people to pitch your services or know those individuals. That's gold when marketing your business.

Over the years, I've used everything from spreadsheets to contact management software to organize my network for marketing efforts. I include all of their standard contact information, including URLs for their social network profiles. It also has been helpful to add reminders of projects we worked on or our business dealings, notes about people they might know who are relevant for my business and even conversation topics to use in future communications. I track the dates, methods of contact, and conversation or message exchange notes in this system.

There's an important lesson I've learned about maintaining a productive and growing network. It's the value of having conversations and brief message exchanges rather than launching into sales type interactions with my contacts. As natural occasions arise to ask for referrals and contract opportunities they're aware of, you seize those. You also can steer conversations in directions to create openings to ask about referrals and contracts.

That said, there may be contacts you know so well that you can make such requests right off. Your long-term or close relationships may give you an edge due to timing, inside information as well as personal endorsements. We trust people whom our close contacts trust.

My one rule in relationships with my contact network is to initially focus on finding ways to help them in some way. The favor is nearly always returned, very often as direct offers to connect me with prospective clients or business opportunities.

For example, I might send a contact a referral, resource, informative article or business lead. Their thank you notes very often include an invitation for them to reciprocate. I rarely would ask for anything right away, but I do follow up with requests when appropriate occasions arise. This mutual assistance strategy pays off and is a sustainable marketing strategy.

When looking for referrals regarding contracting opportunities or connections to contacts, the more specific you are about what you're interested in the better. For example, one of my associates was having little success getting contact referrals from former clients. He offered a wide range of online marketing services and asked for referrals who needed any of those services and in any industry.

I suggested that a better approach might be to focus specifically on one or two of the hottest services—likely the most common pain points for prospects—and one industry that might be ignored by his competition. This is niche marketing rather than a shotgun approach. It helps contacts narrow down possible referrals right from the start.

One of your primary marketing efforts should be to seek referrals to connect with potential clients and find inside tracks to identify available contracts. It's the hidden business opportunity market—similar to the hidden job market—and it's available to you through your contact network.

35
Navigating the Paths of Resistance With Clients

All independent professionals have choices about the types of work, groups of clients to serve and industries to focus on with their business. A pain point comes into play when they must decide to follow either the path of least resistance or pursue a planned direction.

The path of least resistance refers to continuing the same type of work with the same group of clients in the same industry as you've been involved with in the past. A related but slightly different case is when you tend to accept opportunities that arise by default. Many times, it's easy to go with the flow and not fight battles to seek new projects and clients.

For example, let's say you've been employed a project manager in commercial construction for many years. You could let your business replicate that same work, relying on your existing contacts, companies and types of projects. Opportunities likely would surface after you've let everyone know that you're now available independently. If this is the business you want, that's great. If not, you've got to make the effort to move beyond that low hanging fruit to venture into a new, planned use of your project management skills.

A planned direction is focused on intent and specific actions. This is the type of work, group of clients and industry you really want to channel your efforts to serve. In most cases, you can't rely on opportunities just popping up spontaneously.

Using the project manager example again, let's say you want to move into project management for environmental restoration. Now, you likely would need to establish your visibility with a different set of contacts and organizations in this different industry. Your existing contacts certainly could be of assistance if their projects cross into your target market. They might provide referrals to people they know who could use your services. However, this new direction probably demands far more effort to pursue than your previous work. If it's the direction you want to go, it's worth the extra work to seek it.

This isn't an either/or proposition. You can balance these two approaches if you're careful not to diverge from the direction you really want to go. I must admit that I've fallen into the trap of veering toward the path of least resistance several times. I was offered lucrative contracts doing work I previously said I wouldn't do again. Sometimes, it was laziness. Other times, I rationalized it because I was helping out a former client or associate with whom I had a good relationship. While these choices were good for business income, they did distract me from efforts to secure the types of work I very much wanted to pursue. I might have missed great opportunities in my target field while I worked on these easy-to-get projects. I felt a bit of guilt because I wasn't doing what I knew I should be doing.

Many age 50-plus professionals set out on their own because they're burned out of what they've done for many years. The worst thing they could do is end up in the same work, just on their own. So, staying true to one's motivation and vision is key here.

If you're in the early stages of building your business, you might have to accept the path of least resistance to survive. There's nothing wrong with that. But, if you created your business to work in a different field or industry, be sure to not abandon that effort. Stick to the core intent behind your business plan.

Ideally, be all-in whether the path of least resistance is your choice, you plan on building a very different business or a blend of these two approaches makes good business sense.

36
Remembering the Power of Conversations to Build Your Business

Even professionals our age seem to have become less comfortable having conversations, despite that being the more common generalization about Gen-Xers and Millennials.

A business friend exclaimed the other day, "Who talks anymore? And why would I spend time talking with someone without a very specific agenda?" That's a pain point on many levels because such specific conversations rarely build relationships. They tend to eliminate the chance to stumble upon unexpected insights and opportunities barely related or totally unrelated to the narrow topic.

We have adopted text messaging, emails, social network messaging and video calls to quickly say what we want to say or ask questions. Electronic communication is efficient. It's my primary tool for interaction with clients, associates and prospects. The fact is that this level of communication gets business done efficiently.

Yet, I tend to prefer calls and face-to-face meet-ups when possible. Maybe these conversations begin with a fairly specific topic, but then I try to open them up with a business related or personal question. Each week, I make sure that I have at least a couple of unstructured conversations that flow spontaneously in various directions within and outside our particular industries or professions. We ask each other questions and share thoughts about issues we're facing or ideas we've come across. Often, we discuss projects we're working on to get each other's insights. It's not uncommon to mention opportunities we've spotted, as well.

There are two pain points about conversations I'm compelled to address. The first one is not making the effort to set aside time for unstructured business conversations. I've asked some associates how they transitioned back into having these talks. No one could provide any secret to becoming comfortable conversing, other than just deciding to start doing it and remembering how to listen more than talk. However, the most common prompt they found for initiating conversations was running across news and work issues that made them think of particular associates. "I saw this article and thought it related to what you're working on," I might say. In other words, I look for reasons to connect people I know with things I read, see, do and think about—excuses to talk.

The other pain point is the disadvantage of not having general business conversations. There are big benefits to these meaningful exchanges. They help uncover trends, reveal new connections among business ideas, present the chance to have our assumptions and actions questioned, and offer compelling topics to explore. Often, we discover shared interests and even ideas to collaborate on. Conversations aid in networking and in marketing to identify new opportunities. To miss out on enjoying these benefits is a serious disadvantage in business.

I've unexpectedly obtained referrals to new clients and was alerted about projects via general conversations. Some chats have prompted me to change directions on business decisions, saving me time and effort due to erroneous conclusions. I've been introduced to people I might never have met if not for a single idea discussed in passing and someone saying, "I should introduce you to one of my contacts who'd enjoy talking with you about this subject."

If you're uncomfortable starting conversations, here are a few openers I often use:

- I came across this article on [fill in the topic] and wondered what you'd think about it.
- We haven't connected in quite a while, what interesting projects are you working on these days?
- I'm working on a project dealing with [fill in the description] and I'm curious to get your thoughts.

I believe that conversations put humanness back into our business lives. We get to know what and how others think about business topics, what they're curious about and insights they have built on their knowledge and experience. Conversations establish trust, long-term business relationships and valuable communication channels that can be especially helpful for us due to the challenges we face.

So, learn to talk with—not just talk to—others to reap the many benefits. Set aside a half-hour or an hour to converse with a colleague or business contact each week. Ask questions. Explore what's on each other's minds. Listen, learn, be inspired and feel connected.

37
Targeting the "Right" Types of Projects

"Go after every type of project and take what you can get." I've heard that approach far too many times from very experienced businesspeople… and I don't understand. Not only does it sound like working from a position of desperation, which can have negative consequences, but it isn't a sound marketing strategy.

Way too much time will be spent seeking one-off, often low-budget projects that may not even align with the clients and industries you want to work with. It's how many gig workers operate. They focus on the volume of projects—also referred to as churning projects—to try to make a living. Long hours, as in working seven days a week and evenings, just isn't a sustainable business model for any age worker. Quality that's just good enough is okay with many of them and even a great number of their clients.

What are the right types of projects to build a long-term, profitable business? One is repeat clients. These are clients whom you've identified as having ongoing needs for your services. You research these prospects to ensure that they fit your criteria for desirable clients by their industry, work they do related to your services, pain points for which you have solutions and the type of cultures or people you'd like to engage with.

Your goals should be to strategically and persistently find ways to build relationships with these prospects. Once you have the opportunity to work with them on a project, you'll have proven your value as a go-to professional on an ongoing basis. Depending upon the industry and your type of services, there may be a chance to set up a retainer-based arrangement or on-call contract. Otherwise, do what you can to remain visible to them over time to be offered projects as they arise—as a preferred service provider.

This has been the foundation of my business. I have one client for whom I've been an on-call consultant and writer for over 20 years. I was an on-call contractor for another client for about 13 years. Other businesses have been my clients for two years or more. These all started with one project and my expressed interest in being considered for more projects as they arise. I also made sure they knew about my full range of services.

Another important ingredient for business success is to pursue clients with long-term projects. These clients offer projects that range from weeks to months and, occasionally, years. You basically use the same strategy as with repeat clients. However, you target prospects you've researched to know they have lengthy projects or extended contractual engagements. This is no guarantee that you'll identify such prospects easily, so using the repeat client strategy is best.

It's important that you make it known that you're looking for long-term projects and willing to commit to those by adapting your business as is necessary. Yes, that means serving fewer clients and running a certain amount of risk by becoming somewhat dependent upon fewer contracts. Therefore, you must weigh the pros and cons, as well as make a special effort to protect your revenue stream if that long-term contract ends.

I've had long-term contracts and non-contractual commitments for a variety of my services. For some, I set a length of time for my commitment such as one year to establish the work activity or take the project to a certain point. One of my non-contractual projects—was based on an understanding between the client and me—recurred for about two months every year for around 10 years, so I planned other work around it.

I tend to have quite a few big, complex projects that vary from part-time to full-time for periods over several to many months. I've positioned myself with certain companies to be available for these contracts. That said, the reality is that they can occur at any time with little advance notice so there can be some scheduling challenges to resolve.

Ah, what about those high-paying projects? These fall into the subcategory of dream clients we all hope to have, for repeat or long-term projects. The only way I can describe such clients from my experience is very successful businesses or businesspeople who are willing to pay top rates for extraordinary service, quality of work and a high level of expertise.

I've only engaged with these types of clients through referrals, as such projects are rarely advertised. I think that age 50-plus professionals are well-suited to be candidates for high-paying projects due to the top-level experience we provide and our industry connections.

Always be on the lookout for prospects who appear to fit this category and devise strategies to position yourself for work opportunities. You might include a note about your preference for long-term projects in your marketing content. Maybe describe the specific types of projects that fit this category. This also can be one of the ways to differentiate your services from your competition.

38
Spotting Hidden and Subtle Marketing Opportunities

A key to strategic marketing is identifying and acting on opportunities that your competition doesn't look for or see. As an age 50-plus professional, you're well-suited to using this business-building strategy. Your industry knowledge and experience position you to know where and how to spot signs that prospective clients need your assistance.

The pain point is that it's easiest to seek the highly visible opportunities that arise through ads, referrals and other conventional means. It's more complicated to use detective work to reveal hidden opportunities using business-social networks, contacts' blogs and news sources.

The objective is to cultivate relationships with potential clients by initiating interactions. Ideally, these exchanges lead to you to pitch your services for identified needs. You'll only see these opportunities by regularly scanning posts, blogs and news on your social network platforms and by receiving news or reports from relevant industry sources. Note that my reference to social networks means your direct connections as well as contacts through professional interest groups with members representing prospective clients. You must be searching outside communication channels with colleagues in your profession, as most of them aren't your prospects.

The following are some methods my associates and I have used to spot and respond to opportunities:

- Requests for referrals – You may find social network posts with requests for referrals by individuals looking to connect with service providers. Chances are that the posters wish to avoid advertising their needs so they can fast-track their contracting. They trust that referred providers have been vetted by colleagues or contacts. One approach is to respond through private messaging with personal offers to discuss their needs and how your services might be what they're looking for. You can mention that if your services aren't a good fit, you'll try to connect them with someone you know and trust. Little favors build relationships.

- Needs for contract work candidates – You always want to respond to these social network posts via private messages. Include notes about why your services are worth considering and some content that shows you know something about the poster's business. This is a very brief and personalized offer, not an aggressive sale pitch. You are much more likely to get a response if you make this small effort, than by only forwarding your email address or phone number along with the message "contact me" or "I'm interested."

- Implied needs for services – What content in a social network post implies a need for services? An example might be a post that describes an issue a person or business is facing, along with questions or requests for suggestions. This is a chance to provide useful feedback with an offer to discuss it more. That's when you'd mention your services. Again, this usually isn't the place for aggressive selling. Time a soft pitch with a comfortable opening.

- News about rapid company growth – Rapid growth often results in urgent needs for specialized talent, with contract services often being the fastest solution. Use contacts or research to identify the right person to approach. Then, customize your pitch by referring to the specific needs you think they have and your qualifications to help. Frame you pitch around your value during this time of rapid growth.

- Announcements about launches of startups – Essentially, you would use the same approach as with rapidly growing companies. The difference is that the founders likely will feel they cannot afford your level of experience. Also, they might think you won't understand their startup culture. You must specifically address these hurdles. For example, say that you're open to creative payment arrangements such as an incremental fee plan (e.g., low fee to start and increases over time). Cite your previous experience working successfully with startups. Dissolve their doubts right off.

- News about or by companies of interest – By offering substantive comments regarding the posted news on social networks or news publication sites, you may become visible to the company's executives. Also, you can identify company contacts to approach based on the news or even their comments. The types of comments that get noticed include ideas based on your expertise, references to relevant lessons or facts in articles or books, resources related to their news, or offers to connect them with your contacts.

- Posts about promotions of people working in your field – Use congratulations messages to these contacts as excuses to start conversations. That allows to you mention how your services might be of interest to them later. Over the course of conversations, inquire about their work and business to identify pain points.

Always emphasize conversations more than sales, customize pitches citing specific needs and make it personal enough to foster relationships. Remember that these interactions are about their pain points, not about you. Listen, ask questions and seek engagement to turn less visible online opportunities into new business.

39
Building an Effective Professional and Business Platform

Visibility tends to produce opportunities. A drawback for your level of experience as an age 50-plus professional in your particular field is that it likely insulates you from opportunities outside your narrow business circles. This pain point results in your lack of visibility beyond the types of work and audiences of prospects within those circles.

There are simple methods to increase your visibility to attract new business or connect with new audiences who can move you in the directions you want to go. One of the most important ways to accomplish this is to develop a business platform. The components of platforms vary by the industry you work in, the type of work you do and the audiences you wish to reach.

For example, let's say you're a video producer-director who mainly works with advertising agencies on commercials. You'd like to position yourself for opportunities to work on a greater variety of projects, such as producing live events, documentaries, crowdfunding videos, low-budget films, media for e-learning programs and long-form marketing videos. You have the transferable skills and knowledge to successfully handle these projects—maybe even have dabbled in them over your career. Unfortunately, you're known in the advertising community but invisible to these other production and client communities. How do you build a platform that will increase your visibility to such target audiences?

I've known producers-directors who use a variety of activities to develop their platforms. They re-design their Web sites to creatively pitch how their extensive experience in one area of production has prepared them well for the other types of productions they want to tackle. Some have even produced and directed personal projects or took on pro bono work to be able to show examples.

Another platform related strategy they use is to speak to groups who include prospective clients in those new project areas. Writing articles and social network posts on subjects related to new types of projects can help create a regular audience and reach target prospects.

Some producers-directors have even launched creative multi-media marketing campaigns to get on the radar of new target audiences. These included podcasts, series of videos posted on multiple platforms and social networks, crowdfunding efforts for their own or others' projects, their own online magazines, creative email campaigns, engaging mailers, blogs, and hosting of business-social events for face-to-face contact.

Before you head off to create your platform, conduct a little research. Clearly identify the individuals you want to reach, by their job titles, work focus, compatibility in style and clientele, typical budgets, subject matter or products they deal with, and any other factors that ensure you're concentrating on the right audience(s). Next, figure out how to reach them through your platform as part of your marketing efforts. Business-to-business outreach is very different from business-to-end-user. You must indicate how you address their business needs.

Figure out how to get in front of prospective clients' eyes, be listened to, meet in person or be referred to by their trusted associates. Tailor your efforts and methods to sub-groups within your target audiences, if that boosts your visibility.

An additional way to build your platform is to serve as a connector for new and existing contacts. By making introductions, you build relationships but also subtly market yourself by increasing your visibility. This is a big value of the large network you've built over the years. Don't ignore the many ways to benefit from it.

Your visibility platform is not a one-off effort. It's an ongoing campaign tied to your branding. Think of professional speakers who write articles and books, serve as a news experts on-call, appear on TV shows, produce podcasts, create training videos, etc. They're always looking for ways to reach target audiences and expand their followers.

Look at what others in your field do to support their platforms. Try the same strategies and add your unique twists to differentiate your business from the competition.

40
Using Content Marketing to Build Visibility and Sell Your Services

Content marketing is a way to publish useful information, educational and training material, or advice online aimed at target audiences. The goal is to use this communication to build relationships and increase your business' visibility. It's often described as indirect marketing because you're not hard selling or using traditional advertising. You're offering something of value to establish connections that can lead to new business.

Here's the most common pain point. The best content is created from your experience and knowledge, rather than content re-published from others. This means you must learn to be comfortable using one or more of the common content marketing distribution methods. These include writing articles or books, producing your own podcasts (like radio shows) or video-blogging (like TV shows).

Your original content is the most effective type because you can shape the messaging, ensure that it's authentic, communicate with your "voice" so audiences get to know you, and speak directly to prospective clients' interests and needs based on your expertise. As a 50-plus professional, you are perfectly positioned to use content marketing successfully because you can offer valuable information and insights.

For example, your written content may take the form of short or long articles "distributed" on various publishing platforms. These include social networks, a blog on your Web site or a blogging platform, personal content platforms that serve as e-magazines or feature story platforms, Web sites that feature your column or articles, or other online platforms that serve as publishing mediums. Podcasts can be distributed on your Web site, personal podcasting platforms or business themed platforms that feature collections of podcast series from various experts. Video blogs can be distributed on your Web site, general video platforms or business themed platforms that feature collections of video series from experts.

In a way, this is a method of self-syndicating your content. Your writing or recordings appears on channels that your target audiences see or hear. There are many books and online resources for instructions on these various publishing methods. They can provide step-by-step instructions on everything from blogs to articles.

Sharing your wisdom and expertise for free is an effective way to enhance your market position as an expert in your field. Content marketing works for most professional fields and within any industry. The results are incoming inquiries about your services, requests for interviews by others, invitations to speak at events and referrals by your audience members. Your main investment is time. That's unless you need assistance to produce the content or you must pay for a presence on certain platforms. Yet, most of the well-known platforms for writing and media are free to use for distribution of content.

What type of content should you develop? The simple answer is that which addresses the pain points of your target audience with solutions, insights, advice and resources from your knowledge and experience. Industry issues, trends and problems you've faced can be compelling content.

This might sound like you're giving away your services. However, the content you're distributing is not specific to companies, so you're really providing teasers or general suggestions for what you could do for audience members as clients. The strategy is to show them the level of value you have to offer so they hire you for projects.

Your content must resonate with your audiences. It should speak to them as it would from a coach, trusted advisor, educator and industry expert. Personal stories and insights are readable, memorable and attract readers. Just conveying information—like talking to an audience—is not as effective as talking with an audience. Make your content presentation like a conversation, as it would be if the audience members were your clients already. Authenticity is critical. You're giving audiences the virtual experience of collaborating with you as their service provider.

Content marketing works. I've generated a significant amount of business using this strategy, as well as generated referrals from it.

41
Conducting Prospect Research to Increase Pitch and Proposal Success

Far too many age 50-plus professionals waste time and effort pursuing the wrong clients and submitting ineffective pitches. This is despite years of experience and knowing better. Sometimes it's laziness and other times it's due to a lack of confidence in their research skills.

To be clear, the wrong clients are ones who likely don't use your types of services or aren't a good fit for you due to your higher fees and experience level. Ineffective pitches are boilerplates that focus too much on you and not enough on your solutions to the prospects' challenges.

The only way to address this pain point is to identify which prospects to pitch. Then, find ways to customize your pitches by investing the time to research answers to key questions. Begin with questions to uncover the information critical for your decision about whether or not to pitch the prospects. Your goal is to identify prospective clients you can and want to serve for the long-term, a key for your business to be sustainable.

The next set of questions serve as the basis for what to include in your pitches. For example, consider the following questions:

- What would you say if a prospective client asked you what you know about his or her company? (Being specific, beyond generalities about what they do, how big they are, where they're located, etc.)
- How would you describe the prospect's market position, for their products or services, in a way that shows you understand that business?
- What are your impressions of the prospect's products or services?
- What are the prospect's vision and values?
- What sets this prospect apart from their competition and other organizations in general?
- How does this prospect align, in business model and performance, with industry trends?
- What is it about the prospect's communications in blogs, Web content and interviews that make those messages sound authentic and meaningful?
- How do the needs of this prospect align with work you wish to do in the short-term or long-term?
- Why could you feel invested in the success of this prospect over time?
- Why do the leaders and staff connected with your area of work seem like individuals with whom you'd like to work?

The following are my favorite sources to reveal answers to questions like those stated above and other areas:

Prospect's Web site – Review their product or service marketing information, leadership profiles, case studies, blog, news releases, current white papers or reports, career page, and "About us" or company overview content.

LinkedIn – Check the prospect's page for overview information, posts and articles, leaders and employees to whom you are connected, their "See jobs" page for employment needs trends, and Slideshare decks to view their presentations. Also look up profiles of "Similar companies" to know their competition.

Glassdoor – Survey the overview, employee reviews, photos, interviews, updates, awards and jobs for their employment needs and trends. Understand the reviews can be weighted toward the negatives, as is the nature of many rating platforms.

Industry publications and financial publications – Read articles by and about the prospect, quotes from leaders and employees, the most current articles about the prospect's industry and trends, and assessments about the prospect's financial performance.

This approach to research on prospective clients should get you off to a good start selecting better prospects and developing far better pitches. That way, you'll avoid the frustrating pain point of wasting time and effort.

As you gain experience conducting this type of research, you'll identify the most productive ways to uncover valuable details and shortcuts depending on your industry. Use research to give yourself a competitive advantage and impress prospective clients with your insights about them.

42
Developing Proposals for Your Services

I think it's fair to say that developing proposals is one of the most challenging tasks for independent professionals. Although age 50-plus professionals likely have written or processed many proposals over their careers, that experience likely doesn't make writing them any easier. This is an inescapable pain point of being in business for yourself.

Let's address the ageism issue right off. Will stating your years of experience, senior-level professional status or other age-related information on proposals make you non-competitive with prospective clients? While I'm sure this happens, it's not a problem that I'm concerned about.

Presenting a proposal for contract work is quite different than applying for employment. Prospective clients are looking for solutions from professionals whom they believe can deliver and fit their budgets. As long as our skills, knowledge, experience, solutions and overall value are relevant and presented convincingly, we are just as competitive or even more so than others in our fields.

It's important to frame age and experience level related aspects of your value proposition as benefits in proposals. For example, a list of previous projects can reflect your deep experience with similar, successful work. The fact that you've handled many projects over time, especially recently, means that you've kept up in your field and with your services to remain relevant. A proven track record is a powerful marketing tool.

Another persistent pain point with proposals is the time investment. It takes time to prepare effective proposals. It's tempting to minimize that investment of time by taking shortcuts such as using generic or boilerplate proposals with little customization.

I've developed many successful proposals for my services as well as for clients. Also, I've seen many proposals prepared by businesses run by people of all ages and ones from larger companies. The vast majority of these proposals were very general with what looked like a few "blanks" filled in to adapt them to the prospect. This is an incredible waste of time and resources. For self-employed professionals, we just cannot afford to play a numbers game with proposals. We'll end up spending all of our time writing them and not getting paid for our services.

I want to stress two main messages here. First, focus on quality over quantity of proposals. Only propose your services to clients you want to work with as well as for the projects you want and ones you're at least reasonably qualified to handle. This approach alone increases your odds of being awarded contracts.

Second, make your investment of time count. You must conduct some research about prospects to understand who they are, what they do, how they do what they do, their mission, their market position, information related to their pain points and even their history addressing needs related to your type of services. This is the only way you can speak intelligently about their needs and impress them.

You cannot just get proposals out the door to prospects and worry about the specifics of their needs in the interviews. The fact is that you won't get to the interview stage by submitting incomplete and unprofessional proposals. Personalize and customize your proposals. Even offer preliminary ideas for solutions to their pain points. Like in sports, preparation is what produces victories.

Generally, there are two types of proposals: unsolicited offers for your services and submissions in response to requests for proposals (RFPs). Both must be customized via proper research.

For unsolicited proposals, you want to generally sell your services but customize elements for each prospect. Therefore, you should address the prospect's range of pain points that your services (solutions) address and all of your relevant qualifications to show that you're a perfect fit for them.

For RFP submissions, your focus shifts to customizing your content for the specific projects and contexts for your work with that organization. Never submit incomplete RFP documents. Answer every question, fill in every blank entry space and provide every piece of information they request. There's no thinking, "I'll give that to them later" or room for missing elements. Incomplete proposals are deemed non-responsive and you're no longer considered for the contract.

Considerable effort is required to become skilled at developing proposals, even with many years of business experience to rely on. It's important, though, because proposals and pitches will play a major role in determining your success. That also means there are more pain points to talk about.

According to job hunting experts, the value of cover letters is up for debate. Yet, for independent professionals pitching their services via proposals, cover letters can be powerful marketing tools. They give you a chance to quickly convey messages that might not be covered in your resume or CV, capabilities statement or application form. I'd encourage you to use cover letters to accomplish the following:

- Emphasize how your knowledge, skills and experience are especially appropriate with the project.
- Mention information that reflects how much you know about the company and understand their needs.
- Touch on the personal and professional reasons why you want to work with the client and on their project.

Communicate your "why proposition" in the introduction section of proposals. All proposal writers, especially those age 50-plus, should find a way to state their mission or cause. This is why you are in business on a personal level. The reason is there is an emotional element in the hiring of contractors. If your cause aligns with that of the prospect, it frames your services as a good fit with their business vision. Over the years, I've learned that a deciding factor on being awarded many contracts was that the client and I had similar missions. I had to be fully qualified for the work, of course, but that X-factor was an important connection.

A specific pain point that's often ignored is how many ideas or processes to give away in proposals about the solutions you have to offer. Yet, a way to elevate the persuasiveness of a proposal is to provide a taste of initial ideas regarding how you might address a prospect's needs. Such hints show that you've invested significant thought about the prospect and their needs. It's a way to clearly connect the value of your services to their pain points. I've found that these ideas can be great conversation starters in follow-up communications and interviews. This requires some effort, but it can separate your proposal from those of your competition.

One of the most annoying pain points is silence from prospects after submitting a proposal. Your first thought might be that your proposal was rejected and that the prospect is unprofessional and inconsiderate not to respond with that news. Although that might be the case occasionally, you actually don't know what's going on behind the scenes with that proposal recipient or the company. You don't know what you don't know. I've experienced delayed responses to my proposals due to a prospect's sudden personnel issues, budget changes, company mergers and acquisitions, changes in needs, and other factors.

Occasionally I followed up with my contact by email or phone to check on the status of my proposal and learned the reason for the delay on a decision. Other times, I just moved on with other work until I heard back. I rarely experienced permanent silence. And in several cases, I was contacted as long as months after my submission when they were ready to move forward on the contract. The important lesson is not to jump to conclusions when you don't hear back about submissions.

My last and maybe most important message about proposals is the importance of learning from successes and failures. It's frustrating to make the effort to prepare great proposals and not win those contracts. Too many times we don't know why we didn't win. Many contracting managers hesitate to explain their reasons to you due to the risk of disclosing something that could expose them to complaints or lawsuits. For this reason, I try to learn as much as possible about why I had successes. My clients have been very open about specific factors for their decisions. Pick an appropriate time and just ask. That information could help you refine your proposal development.

If you're concerned that your proposal writing is not in top form, seek assistance from an experienced proposal writer or take a course on proposal writing. Another option is to have someone familiar with marketing communications take a look at a few of your proposals to offer some feedback.

Proposals reflect your professionalism, competence and desire to work with prospects. Make them great.

43
Selling Your Soft Skills Along With Your Expertise

Clients want effective solutions from an experienced professional like you. They need your knowledge, skills and experience—your job-specific hard skills—to address their pain points. However, in the past several years I've learned that my clients have begun to appreciate qualities beyond the hard skills normally associated solely with being qualified for types of work. Those "other" qualities are called soft skills.

Soft skills often are described as qualities associated with interpersonal skills and professionalism. These include communication skills, listening skills, empathy, creative thinking, problem-solving, critical thinking, time management, decision-making, flexibility and adaptability, as well as motivation and teamwork skills.

Our pain point as service providers is that soft skills are challenging to reflect in capabilities statements, resumes and proposals. To just say that you have a checklist of soft skills somehow doesn't come across as credible because they're not measurable or concrete like hard skills. It's easiest to show your strengths and authenticity related to soft skills during personal interactions, such as interviews, live pitches, conversations and project discussions.

One of the best ways to do this is through stories. By this, I mean stories of projects you've worked on, organizations you've worked with, professional growth you've experienced or industry issues to which you've given considerable thought.

How did you manage challenges? What interesting experiences did you have working with clients or colleagues? How have you coped with successes and failures? Why have your written about certain subjects? Notice how questions like these get to who you are as a person and as a professional. They also are indicators of how you communicate and collaborate with others.

Stories that touch on these characteristics may be included in cover letters, introductions in proposals, case studies of projects you've worked on, your Web site content, content marketing activities and anywhere else you present your services. Be careful not to make this content over-the-top personally or emotionally like the over-sharing we see too often on social networks. It's business information on a humanistic level. After all, a big part of hiring decisions is emotional—that part of the nebulous area called fit.

The trick that I've used to provide prospective clients with an impression of my soft skills is to arrange preliminary conversations. Yes, we discuss the project and the services I can provide. But, I always try to frame some of what I say within the context of soft skills.

For example, I'll bring up my experience with a project similar to the one the prospect needs addressed. My snapshot description won't just present the facts such as I did this to solve that and these were the measures of success. I'll touch on the process that took place, with its challenges, interactions with others and how issues were resolved to be able to express soft skill aspects.

Another area that touches on soft skill characteristics is to relay thoughts about the similarity of your business missions, customer service commitment or connections to your communities. This is something you could do in your introductory emails or messages.

Of course, I'd suggest that you only approach prospects for whom you feel highly qualified to do the work. Your business marketing materials and resources should effectively present information that supports your qualifications. However, an important complement to that is the personal, professional outreach related to your soft skills.

Devise creative ways you can integrate your soft skills in your marketing efforts. I believe you'll have a competitive advantage over those who don't understand the importance of these skills and how they affect hiring decisions.

44
Standing by Your Value Proposition

It's easy to question the value of your skills, knowledge and experience, especially at age 50-plus. This may be when work becomes scarce, a major client is lost or we feel burned out of providing certain services. This is one of the dangerous pain points that can paralyze you, so you stop doing the work that you must do to stay afloat.

This can be the case when preparing to launch your business. Self-doubts creep in. You might start imagining negative scenarios of what could happen. That's when it's time to step back from the emotional minefield. Instead, think about why you decided to become an entrepreneur and your credentials that support your decision.

First off, your value as perceived by prospective clients often depends on the quality of the solution(s) you're offering. The more impact your solutions can have with a client, the more your work will be valued. Can you save them significant time, money, resources or prevent problems? Will you help them make more money, attract better employees, better engage customers, work more efficiently and effectively, increase their business', improve their products, help them create something new, etc.?

Those questions present your value proposition. Consider looking at your business from the perspective of your past satisfied clients or work and those who respect your work. That way, you know how valuable you'll continue be to your present and future clients.

Another entrepreneurial mindset regarding your value has to do with who you are as a professional. Don't underestimate the skill set you have to offer. Your previous job titles likely don't reflect all of the services you actually provided.

For example, a sales representative does far more for a company than just seek out and secure transactions. The job includes functions such as customer feedback curator, the company's face in the industry (e.g., industry relations and marketing), product development consultant, industry networker, trend analyzer, business communications specialist, project manager, sales event producer, conference speaker, opportunity spotter and personnel recruiter. These are all marketable services, individually and as a service package. Again, this is more evidence that you offer great value.

If you need an exercise to better recognize your professional value, make a list of every function you've had in your career. After completing your list, cluster the skills you want to emphasize as your primary business services. Match those services to the pain points of your prospective customers, as you'd define them in your business plan. The fact that you offer those solutions to known needs of prospective clients means that you clearly offer value.

All of this should help reassure you that you have professional value that others will pay for. It's why they'll trust you to solve their problems. And it's why you can feel confident that you've launched a viable business.

Remember that it'll be very difficult to get others to appreciate your value if you don't believe in your value.

45
Pitching Services to Clients at Interviews and Meetings

What's your story about your services and how you can solve clients' problems? What will they gain from hiring you? Can you tell your story in a way that engages prospects and is meaningful from their perspective, not just yours?

Despite our years of business experience, a pain point is that our work hasn't necessarily equipped us with the skills to tell these stories effectively or comfortably. This is person-to-person sales. We may not like the sales aspects of self-employment but our ability to handle this role likely will be the difference between success and failure.

Preparation is the key to feeling confident pitching your services. In other words, you need to start by knowing your audience, anticipating their questions and being crystal clear about how your specific services can solve their problems. Then, you're prepared to open a conversation with them that leads to further discussion or being hired.

For example, I was contacted about a project by a company for which I had worked a couple years prior. I first communicated with this new project manager via a phone call. She described the project and asked me to come to her office to discuss it and my services. Prior to that, I conducted some research on their client and the subject matter.

During the interview, she asked me if the project seemed like a good fit. I described my experience with a similar project, including how I addressed some challenges my team faced. I mentioned several points that showed I knew about the customer's operations related to the project as well as some pain points our end product would address. Then, I suggested a few ideas on how we could handle this project.

My final thoughts included the fact that I worked as a contractor with her company previously and what my rates were for these types of services. That seemed to cover everything she wanted to discuss. I took that opportunity to ask her some questions about the customer's team, special aspects with this project, the level of creative freedom we'd have, our team members and the set-up for our contract.

This approach is quite different than how many contractors focus on pitching their experience and skills. Too often, they talk only about themselves rather than about the prospective clients and their needs. I've had far more success pitching clients when I concentrate on their pain points through the lens of my experience, skills and services. It really is all about them.

In this example, I began by assuring her I was qualified for this work and that I was experienced in solving problems typical for such projects. Then, I made it clear that I was knowledgeable about her customer and sensitive to issues that might arise. This implied that I appreciated the importance of this project to them. To reflect my strong interest in this work, I provided initial ideas regarding our collaboration on aspects specific to this project. I also casually reminded her of my previous contracts with her company and established my current rate. Finally, by asking her several questions I proactively shifted the conversation to our business relationship.

What I was doing was answering my prospective client's questions in advance of her actually having to ask them herself. She gave me the opportunity to do this easily by her general opening question. But, I could have done the same thing if she asked something else. I would have answered that question, then pivoted right into our conversation. Admittedly, I did have the advantage of knowing about a project and customer in advance.

What if this were a general interview during which you'd be pitching a variety of services? I'd suggest that all of your preparation be shifted to her company and the types of projects you'd likely be hired to handle. So, you might focus on recent projects they handled, if you know about them via their Web site or other research, and pain points you think they might be facing. You'd want to make clear connections between their needs and how your skills, knowledge and experience would apply to address them. Again, the pitch would be about her company and its needs within the context of how your services would be relevant.

46
Coping With Age Bias During Interviews

No matter whether prospective clients interview us by phone, video call or in-person, the age issue tends to arise in subtle and not so subtle ways. This is a pain point that's unavoidable. The exception would be if you could tell from the opening communication with the prospect that their key decision factor was your professional value, with your years of experience being an asset.

One case is if you're being interviewed for a contract by a procurement manager who's around age 50. This should be an advantage, right? In many cases our experience is appreciated more by peers. However, the reverse can occur too. Even older managers can believe that certain projects are better suited to younger contractors based on common biases. They might think that it's worth sacrificing experience to better align them with current trends or reach younger demographics. This seems especially unfair due to the age of the interviewer, but it's the reality we face.

Another case is when you're interviewed by procurement managers who are significantly younger. Their biases may or may not be obvious. You can pitch your position as being the right person with the right skills and knowledge to tackle the project successfully. But, if they've made up their minds, you're probably not going to change them.

On the other hand, these managers could be more interested in your expert services than your age. They might even acknowledge the advantage of contracting with someone who doesn't need much supervision or how deep experience is exactly what they need. In my experience with cases like this, the discussion moves quickly into details about their project and my availability based on the timeline and scope of work.

There have been few occasions when I could tell that the interview was over when I walked into the office just by the managers' facial expressions. Other times, there were not so subtle hints by the questions asked and phrasing of comments by that manager about the project, team or company culture. For example, "I'm concerned about this project being a good fit for your skills." Or a creative one was, "With your amazing experience, you could be the CEO of this company rather than work on our project."

As I've said, there are many instances when you won't be able to change the interviewer's mind. There's no reason not to give it a shot, though. If you sense the cultural fit barrier being the key, you can offer a brief story about how well you collaborated with a younger team on a previous project and the types of efforts you employed to make it work. If there seems to be concern about how current your skills are relative to the project, you can describe recent training you've had or summarize a recent project that required current skills and knowledge.

The key is to mitigate concerns or barriers with clearly, concisely and confidently presented evidence and a supporting argument for the benefits you offer. Projecting your energy, interest in the project and company, likable personality, and professionalism can go a long way to deflect age related issues and clinch a deal.

One additional pain point that can be connected to age and experience regards your rates. If the interview is more about negotiating your fees because of your professional experience, you've got to establish solid justification for those fees. You can base your argument on the market rates for your types of services and level of experience, as well as the demands of the project. Consider emphasizing the value that you offer, specifically for the project and the company. Touch on the various benefits of you working on their project.

For example, there's extra value working with a contractor who is accustomed to preventing problems and solving them effectively, proposes ideas to reduce costs associated with projects, offers ways to multipurpose or get more value out of projects, and has associated skills or experience that can benefit the project and company.

You want to flip concerns about the cost of doing business with someone of your age and experience to the advantages of hiring a professional who will do the job extremely well the first time, on time and on budget. If necessary, you also can counter cost concerns with a comparison to the higher fees charged by large firms.

47
Completing Online Contract Applications

Online contract applications can be minefields for age 50-plus professionals due to intentional or unintentional built-in ageism. Plus, there are associated assumptions about skills, knowledge and cost.

In a conversation I had with an associate about his frustration with online contract applications, he brought up the same questions I've asked myself when crafting responses, such as:

1. If I describe my experience and it's obvious that I've worked in this field for many years, will I immediately be rejected as overqualified?

2. If I've worked on projects that are only somewhat similar to the opportunity presented, will the contracting manager still see that my overall qualifications position me well for their project?

3. If I identify when I graduated from college or cannot list recent courses I've taken, will I be rejected due to the assumption that I'm not current with what's being taught to students today?

4. If I state my typical rate for a particular type of work and am not allowed to explain the value that represents, am I setting myself up to be uncompetitive with other applicants?

5. If I hold back on disclosing information that might trigger rejection of my applications, will contracting managers just gather that age-related information on my social network profiles anyway?

The answer to all of these questions is, maybe. It's not like there's any standard online review process or criteria for contractors across all industries. Every company handles contractor selection differently, using different online platforms and candidate management systems.

After my chat with that associate, I asked a sampling of other associates I knew who frequently applied for contracts online. The consensus was that they found little value in hiding or understating information related to age or experience.

In fact, they reminded me how contracting managers and procurement staff often consider candidates differently than human resources and recruitment staff. Because contractors are hired for specific projects or defined time periods, there's far more emphasis on the level of services and desired outcomes. Company culture and other factors can come into play, but not nearly as much as with new hires.

There's also general acceptance by established companies that highly qualified contractors charge more for their services. For example, a regionally known business keynote speaker might charge $8,000 but a nationally known one might command $20,000 or more due to fame and perceived value. Hiring 10 less qualified speakers at $2,000 each like they might do in job hiring just doesn't offer the same value as contracting with the top-level speaker.

What's the best approach when pitching your services via online applications? As much as possible, emphasize the value you have to offer. This means your qualifications and solutions for those particular prospects. It's all related to your years of experience and how you can blend that with current knowledge to solve problems that clients face today.

This may seem obvious but be sure to answer every question and provide everything asked for when completing online applications. You can't assume that you'll be given the chance to provide information later at an interview or second step of their process. There have been several occasions during interviews with prospective clients when they said that I was the only applicant who fully completed the application. What? Yes, that was good for me. But, I felt sorry for what likely would have been qualified candidates making such a fatal mistake. What a waste of time—to not even be considered for the contract due to being deemed "unresponsive."

Always be meticulous when filling out those online applications. Also, consider every piece of information you provide and the language you use as subtle or direct marketing messaging. Think strategically about all of the information you enter so it frames your qualifications and value in the best ways for the project.

48
Engaging Matchmaking Agencies for Contract Work

There are thousands of staffing, placement, recruiting, temp agencies and other organizations that connect contractors with businesses for work locally, regionally, nationally and internationally. I've applied for inclusion on many contractor matchmaking services starting back at around age 45.

At first, some staffers were quite enthusiastic about being able to connect with me as a senior level professional in my field. I even received a few calls about possible contracts. However, I never have been awarded a contract this way.

Although no one admitted specifically that age was a factor, the issue about me being over-qualified did come up. Even more frequently was the barrier of cost. My minimum hourly rate was significantly higher than what they felt their clients would approve.

This marketing option clearly is a pain point for age 50-plus professionals. Contractor matchmaking is a highly competitive business and there tends to be an emphasis on getting placements made as quickly as possible. This means avoiding more complicated placements or cases when the staffing agent must make an extra effort to convince clients to spend more than they intended to do on a contractor.

For example, I was alerted about a long-term contract with an organization that, by coincidence, was one of my former directly hired contract clients. The placement was being handled by a respected local staffing firm. The project involved exactly the same work I performed regularly for that client over about a two-year period. It was clear that I would be the most qualified candidate possible for this contract. I had the proven skills, organization and industry knowledge, history with that project area and even contacts within the organization to facilitate my work there.

A while after my on-call contract came to an end with this organization, I was contacted by a project manager there requesting me to perform the same work again. I was told this was due to my strong track record, knowledge about the work as well as internal recommendations. My experience in this technical area was said to be critical.

I told the staffing firm's agent what my minimum rate would be. There was silence. I said that this was the rate I was paid there for this same work for two years even though that was several years ago. I mentioned that I could even provide documentation to verify my rate and experience with this project. The agent said she would need to talk with a supervisor.

A day or so later, I received a call from the agent. She respectfully acknowledged my superior positioning for the contract but… her supervisor determined that their client probably expected to pay only one-third my rate. One-third the rate that client actually paid me previously for this same project. I mentioned the complex demands of the project and how it would be unlikely that someone qualified to do the work up to the organization's standards would accept such a low rate. They respectfully declined to forward my information to the client.

My associates have reported everything similar experiences. Several describe how they were "ghosted"—no communication whatsoever—after contacting these agencies. Others have had great success being matched with great clients. There are certain professional services that fit the agency model better than others, such as technical writers for documentation and instructional work, software programming specialties, technical human resources functions and types of business operations specialists.

When using an agency to enhance your marketing, I suggest you find one that specializes in your field and is positioned to place senior level and higher hourly rate professionals. The most prominent agencies I'm aware of that represent senior level professionals emphasize employment only, rarely contracting. However, there's no harm in doing some research to find an agency that's a good fit for your experience level, rates and types of services. Ideally, it focuses on serving your target markets.

Be wary about signing exclusive agreements with agencies. Also, be careful of agreements that limit in any way your rights to pursue work outside their service. It would require an extraordinary guarantee of performance on their end to make an exclusive contract even worth considering. Would any agency even offer such a promise?

An interesting development related to this topic is that we're seeing increasingly frequent reports of talent shortages, changes in workforce hiring trends and hints of rebounding interest in older talent. This points to a promising opportunity for agencies that might serve age 50-plus professionals. I think such niche agencies will arise, possibly soon. They would be a helpful component of our marketing strategies.

49
Deciding to Use Online Freelancing Platforms

Highly experienced professionals likely will experience a lot of pain points with online freelance and contracting platforms.

A few years ago, I decided to start giving some these platforms a try. I signed up to be listed on around 10 of the most popular free platforms or ones for which I received free credits to try out their services. I'd say that half of them covered nearly every type of job, ranging from management consulting and graphic design to dog walking and window cleaning. Others focused more on professional services for businesses and organizations.

What have been my findings for this ongoing experiment? My records indicate that I've applied or submitted proposals for 75 to 80 contract projects. Probably three-quarters of the projects were listed by individuals without obvious business entities identified. The balance of them were clearly by representatives of companies or organizations.

This has resulted in only a handful of contracts so far. Surprisingly, two were through platforms that are matchmakers for every type of service. Those were posted by individuals, not businesses. Several other contracts were via platforms strictly for business-to-business services. A couple of projects were months-long and profitable with good clients—an individual and a large company. One little project was for a small business. Another project was for a new non-profit organization for which I decided to provide pro bono services and fee-based work later on.

Interestingly, I was chosen for two projects after those clients had bad experiences with low-cost service "professionals." I suspect that I've been rejected for the vast majority of other projects because my estimated fees were above their budgets. That's because I only submitted applications or proposals when my qualifications were strong matches with their needs and industries.

I've been rejected by two business matchmaking platforms that tout their extensive screening processes to ensure that only highly experienced professionals are invited to work through them. Judging by their cultural fit type questions that clearly targeted younger age groups and the photos of current contractors reflecting almost no age diversity, I'd surmise that there's some pervasive age bias in their processes. Several of my associates have reported similar experiences with these and other "highly selective" platforms.

Probably the biggest challenge with matchmaking platforms for business services is that they're better suited to less experienced freelancers, gig or side hustle workers. In other words, for career transition workers, part-timers and those who are really looking for full-time jobs but freelancing to generate some income.

Workers living in low-wage countries who can charge cut-rate fees have a big advantage with most platforms. This is not to say there aren't talented people out there making money via these platforms. However, this online marketplace is driven more by lowest cost and fast turnaround than by quality and long-term contractor-client relationships.

Speed is the operative word here. To compensate for very low fees, workers must finish projects extremely quickly so quality and customer service rarely are maintained at that pace. Also, many of these workers are putting in 60, 70 and even 80 hours a week to earn minimal incomes.

The other major shortfalls of these platforms include: (1) lack of adequate details to develop valid proposals, (2) confusing descriptions of the services needed, (3) unrealistically low budgets, (4) requirements to pay proposal submission fees just to ask questions to prospects, and (5) alerts about projects that have nothing to do with the services listed in the freelancers' profiles. Most of the projects listed are one-offs, so that puts more pressure on freelancers due to the unstable revenue. Some platforms also have complaints from contractors who couldn't get paid or had their work rejected by clients with no reason or available recourse.

From my experience, I'd say the vast majority of project matchmaking platforms have very limited value for experienced age 50-plus professionals. Networking, referrals and strategic marketing are a far more productive. I do anticipate that improved online marketplaces will emerge for older, experienced professionals to serve businesses that demand quality, value and long-term relationships over lowest cost and quickest turnaround only.

50
Competing to Win Contracts With Government Agencies

Bring up the topic of government contracting with a group of age 50-plus professionals and brace yourself for an outpouring of stories ranging from nightmares to business-saving miracles. The reason for this, from my experience, is because government contracting is unique and challenging in many ways. In other words, there are plenty of pain points for those who choose to pursue government contracts.

I've had mixed success with government contracting over the last 30 years. Along the way, I've been awarded very profitable long-term and individual project contracts with federal agencies as well as a handful of local governments. This work has involved a wide range of my services and even drawn me into new types of services that helped me to expand my client market outside the government realm.

Then again, I've failed to be awarded contracts many times. This was despite the fact that, as I learned later through a bit of research, my proposed team or I was the most qualified applicant. Most times, there was no way to understand the reasoning behind scores for the components of proposals or why another firm was selected with "all things being equal." Other times, their decisions were made strictly on the lowest cost.

First, if you haven't pitched your services to a government entity, you must know that requests for proposals (**RFPs**) usually are required for government agencies at all levels when the dollar amounts of the contracts exceed certain thresholds. RFPs detail the project, scope of work, vendor requirements and qualifications, schedule and other information about the project. You bid your services and cost based on this information, occasionally with additional details from conference calls, pre-bid meetings and supplemental documentation.

Developing proposals is time-consuming, so it's expensive for any small business. Competition for awards usually is tough, due to the number of bidders and the likelihood that you're up against experienced specialists in your category. High-quality proposals put you in the game, but other factors for awards leave every attempt up to a certain amount of chance.

I'm compelled to mention some important realities about government contracting from my experience and off-the-record conversations with government contracting and procurement specialists. Here are some of my thoughts:

- Previous contracts with the agency and for similar projects count big time. Additionally, former agency employees turned contractors often have an inside track for contract awards. Fair or not, these factors can be significant competitive disadvantages for even the most qualified applicants.

- Government agencies usually require certain levels of business insurance, residency requirements, hiring and sub-contracting restrictions, registrations with government vendor-procurement databases, data security specifications, the need to operate as a corporation, and a host of other technical requirements to qualify for awards. These may add overhead costs, limit how you might fulfill contracts, require legal counsel or any number of issues that would make contracts unaffordable to pursue.

- To even know about many contracts and respond before deadlines, contractors often need to be signed up for notices from a central federal government system, individual agencies, state procurement systems and local government contract alert lists. Otherwise, you must regularly scan multiple online RFP opportunity platforms for appropriate contracts.

- Proposal scoring looks like an objective process, but subjectivity plays a role, despite the frequent use of averaged scores from multiple evaluators. Opinions, personal and professional bias and other factors affect scoring.

- There are occasions when RFPs are issued only due to the requirement to do so, as preferred contractors already have been identified. There is no way to know when this is the case.

- Some agencies maintain preferred vendor lists, in which applications are submitted to establish pre-qualified status for approved vendors. This may be announced by RFPs or you must inquire. Just being on the lists doesn't guarantee that your services will ever be requested or that you'll have an opportunity to submit proposals.

My four most important tips for increasing your success with government contracting are: (1) only focus on RFPs that align very well with your qualifications and project experience, (2) answer all questions and respond to every requirement in your proposals even if they don't seem to apply to your business to prevent disqualification by being deemed "unresponsive," (3) be persuasive about how well you understand the project and the function of the agency, and (4) in cover letters, include ideas and content that set you apart from your competition.

51
Using Project Wrap-Ups and Post-Mortems as Marketing Opportunities

The end of a project can be the beginning of a long-term business relationship, if you wrap it up properly. There's the pain point for too many age 50-plus professionals. They send final thank-you messages by email and submit their last invoice. That's it.

The end of a project should be the opportunity to conduct a post-mortem and wrap-up, with the detail level in line with the size of the project. A short or small project deserves a couple of paragraphs to cite what went well, any valuable lessons learned and what could be improved the next time you work together. A bigger or longer-term project contains this same content in more depth, along with relevant data on the process and maybe recommendations for follow-up by the client.

In all cases, some language in the write-ups should reflect your work in a way that connects you more deeply to the client than just in terms of this one-off project. For example, there may be a place to include phrases such as, "The next time we collaborate on a project like this…" You're trying to convey the message that you want to work more with the client as well as the benefits you see in the relationship.

Another important action to take at the end of a project is to do what seems obvious but rarely is done by contractors: ask if a similar project is planned. There is no better time to position yourself for a follow-on project or new one than at the tail end of a successful engagement.

It's tough for most of us to ask a question like this, as it's so sales oriented. One way to make it easier to ask is to personalize it. For example, "I really enjoyed working with you on this project and we achieved great results. If there are other projects in the works with which I could assist you, I'd appreciate the opportunity to develop a proposal for you." Remember that contractor-client relationships are just that, relationships. An open communication channel, previously earned trust and past mutual success with work provide an effective opportunity to secure more contracts.

A twist on the previous strategy of asking about more work is to request an internal referral. This involves asking your client if he/she is aware of appropriate projects that are being launched by colleagues and if you could be introduced to those project leads. Internal referrals like this are very powerful. You enter project discussions with a direct or implied endorsement, already being in the procurement and accounting system, and having proven knowledge of the company's business. I've landed many contracts this way, especially with projects that wouldn't have been advertised.

Your final couple of communications with clients also should ensure that they know about your other services. They probably only know you for the expertise you just provided so they might not think beyond that. With your inside knowledge, you should be aware of two or three potential applications of your other services with their business.

I make sure clients are aware of my full range of services right from the start of projects. However, reminders at the end have successfully prompted offers for follow-on or new projects.

I look at the end of one project as the beginning of ongoing communication with clients, as long as we had a good relationship. My emails or occasional calls include a brief reference to the past projects just to help them remember who I am. I prefer not to make these sales calls. My comfort zone is to frame this type of communication as staying in touch, sharing information that might be of interest to my former clients or alerting them to potential opportunities.

The soft-sell component is just something like, "I look forward to working with you again soon. Please let me know if you'd like to chat about a project or have me submit a proposal." I never directly ask if they have work for me.

Even though we're very experienced in our work and client relations, it's easy to let end-of-project marketing opportunities slip by. We all know how it's far easier to sell past or existing clients on using our services again than it is to acquire new clients. That fact should make this bit of sales more palatable.

FINAL THOUGHTS

52
Moving Beyond Pain Points to Success

My goal in writing this book was to address the many pain points that my associates and I have experienced during our long careers along with effective workarounds for those challenges. I'd like to close with three final thoughts regarding our unique position in the marketplace:

1. The external and self-imposed barriers age 50-plus professionals face as entrepreneurs can be successfully overcome. We can't quickly change many of the external barriers, such as the inequities and the unfairness of ageism, because they're ingrained in many business cultures and individuals' behaviors. However, our successes and actions can't move the dial until our value is recognized, appreciated and eventually sought-after.

   The fastest barriers to eliminate are the self-imposed ones, related to staying relevant, operating and marketing in smart ways, maintaining the right attitude, appreciating your value, and effectively using the assets and resources we have due to our experience and knowledge. If you're driven by a cause, a personal mission embodied by your business, then you can find a way to reach your entrepreneurial goals.

2. The most important forces behind your success as an age 50-plus professional are your levels of adaptability, resiliency and resourcefulness. You must respond to and anticipate your

industry's trends as well as market conditions so that you are positioned to constantly adapt to change.

A key defense is to diversify your services and sources of revenue. Regarding resiliency, you know that projects, marketing efforts, experiments with services and business relationships fail. This is a fact of life for entrepreneurs. Extract the lessons learned, improve what you do and how you do it, and move on. Some efforts and relationships may have failed but that doesn't mean you, personally, are a failure.

Lastly, the amazing attributes you have to uncover paths to success in business are your experience, skills and knowledge. And a key behind these is resourcefulness. You've seen, done and know a lot. That means you have the problem-solving and critical thinking skills to creatively connect the dots to break through or maneuver around obstacles. In addition, you can devise ways to repurpose skills and knowledge to address the needs of different clients and industries, develop new services, and solve problems by reframing them in imaginative ways.

3. You may not fully appreciate the powerful network of colleagues, former clients and contacts you have from your years of business life experience. Helping these people to be more successful inevitably will help you, often in unexpected ways.

   Make time for conversations with members of your network. This can yield new connections with their contacts, opportunities you never would have known about, assistance with challenges you face and encouragement when you need it most. After all, business really is about relationships.

One other point I'd like to make. You don't have a "use by" date on your career. Entrepreneurship can extend your career as long as you wish by using every workaround at your disposal. There is great value in your skills, knowledge and experience and there are many pain points that your prospective clients need you to address.

You can be the professional your clients choose to ensure that their projects are completed on time, on budget, the highest quality, with someone they'd love to work with many more times. As an age 50-plus professional, you are just getting started on a meaningful and profitable journey. All my best for great success in your solo or micro business.

53
Additional Advice and Insights From Experts Around the Globe

The following insights, advice and thoughts have been generously contributed to this book by my inspiring network of business contacts. They are career coaches, business consultants, entrepreneurs, authors/speakers specializing in career development, futurists, mentors, instructors and startup advisors.

Quotations have been grouped by general topics. You'll find detailed profiles for each contributor at the end of this chapter. I encourage you to follow their informative posts and articles via their Web sites and social media. Many have written outstanding books, produced podcasts and videos, as well as have created courses that are relevant to age 50-plus entrepreneurs.

Note: UK spelling has been retained in quotes from my British, Australian and Canadian contributors. Also, the views and opinions expressed in this chapter are those of the authors (my contacts) and do not necessarily reflect my positions on the topics addressed.

Adaptability

Younger people, who have largely grown up during the technological revolution take this need to accommodate and even precipitate disruption for granted. But for older generations—the baby boomers especially—it was easy to become complacent about the status quo in their early careers. The current constant demand to manage change is not second nature to many of them, including even the youngest members of that set who are still in their mid- to late-fifties and have a decade or so of working life yet ahead of them. Many of them find their skill set antiquated and keeping up with rapidly evolving technology difficult. Some experience late-career layoffs and confront the reality of ageism when seeking new, conventional employment. Essentially, they are aging out of the workforce, even while still desiring or needing to work. — Whitney Johnson

Ageism

It's true, if you're 50-plus looking for a full-time job then you might face a bit of ageism but that's if you are looking for something traditional. But, if you're a 50-plus entrepreneur then you have just as much opportunity as the young 20-year-old. In fact, you might have an even better opportunity since you have more life and work experience, not to mention the business contacts! Being an entrepreneur isn't an "age thing," it's a "mindset" thing. Thanks to technology, older entrepreneurs can just as easily connect with communities, build their own person brands, and find gigs on [project/contract matchmaking] sites. — Jacob Morgan

Attitude

Having the right mindset is half the battle, because the first person you have to convince of your value is actually yourself. Once you're comfortable with the idea of unapologetically marketing who you are without getting hung up on your age, the easier you will make it for others to believe in you. — Joseph Liu

Typically, what I find is that many people sell themselves short. Meaning they do not maintain a conviction of what they can truly accomplish. It's easy to say you have left things too late, or you do not have the right experience, or you are too old, but they are just stories in your mind. So, the number one thing you need to do is break free of your old self—your old paradigms. While it may have gotten you where you are so far, you now need to re-invent yourself and that starts with what I call the need to "rewire" your mind. — Dr. Ross McKenzie

This is the time in our lives when we can look back at all the things we've done, including the mistakes we've made and the lessons we've learned, and come up with a way to distill all of our experience into a value proposition that we bring forward. No one wants to hear about the past. Our experience is nice, but by itself is meaningless if it can't help solve a problem someone's having today or are going to be having tomorrow. — John Tarnoff

Branding

[The desire to re-brand and re-launch a career] isn't unique to people 50+, but be sure to be very selective about the value you're now trying to offer. Hone in on one specific area of domain expertise where you can credibly build your personal brand, then ensure all your services and activities consistently reinforce that area of expertise. As someone with significant experience, you are also uniquely qualified to position yourself as a seasoned professional who can offer well-informed insights that only come after spending years in a particular industry. — Joseph Liu

Competitive Advantage

What is a definite disadvantage in the corporate working world is a real advantage when you're in the entrepreneurial world. Because many of the same corporate employers that will not even consider hiring you at age 55 will buy services from you and experiences from you. And as a matter of fact, they'll pay you well because you have the experience. — Jeffrey Wayman Williams

Differentiation

The 50+ professional naturally develops implementation-ready outcomes, action-oriented results. They have been there or they can confidently project forward... and the astute employer knows that. Yes, the fresh-faced MBA may come up with great answers too, but can they be implemented and will the employer sign on for the required actions? — John Groarke

How can self-employed freelancers, consultants, and contractors differentiate themselves from others? By clearly, creatively, and comprehensively outlining what they bring to the table (i.e., their overall, unique and special qualifications) in relation to achieving their client's objectives and meeting their interests. — Greg Hansen

[Age] 50+ consultants are more likely to have knowledge of "old school" industries, for example, manufacturing. Their life experience and maturity also make them well-equipped to help clients manage major organisational change. — Sharon Melamed

Direction

To reinvent ourselves, we are well served to draw from our unique personal reflections and perspective on the world as a way of distinguishing ourselves in this new phase of our lives. Even if we have worked our entire lives in one company or one field, our struggles and triumphs in getting to our current situation forms a narrative that allows us to connect with others, and establish a reinvented path based on both skills and persona. — Joe Wasylyk

Entrepreneurship

When starting out: (1) Find a mentor. Who do you know who might be able to guide you along your new path? You may have to study marketing, finance and employment law. Sign up for a community college or certification program to get the necessary skills. You can begin by contacting your town's or county's Small Business Development Center; (2) surround yourself with a useful board of advisers—a brain-trust. A dynamic board early in your company's life adds gravitas. Those advisers can be formidable references for you with an investor. They can guide you and they may lead you to your first customers; (3) do the job first. Volunteer or moonlight to see if this is a business that is more than a hobby and something that you would truly enjoy on a daily basis and (4) get financially fit. Do a budget. Where can you trim back? If you are starting your business, you may not be able to pay yourself for a year or so as you invest back into the business. You don't want to start tapping retirement funds. Money is the biggest stumbling block to starting a business. And, importantly, debt is a dream killer. — Kerry Hannon

Entrepreneurship offers an avenue to productive, rewarding career continuation for many 50+ workers. By strategically adopting the accelerants of personal disruption, they can remain relevant and attractive even to clients who are much younger. By tapping their distinctive strengths, looking for a genuine problem that people need to solve and moving into that niche, being willing to step back in terms of compensation and/or prestige, battling constraints with resourcefulness and persevering when failure looms, a second career of entrepreneurship can be a great success. Being proactive through personal disruption can help us become change embracers rather than change-resistant. This is an essential attitude and skill to remain in demand in the modern workplace. — Whitney Johnson

For me, having a successful corporate career does not mean the same skills will translate to be a successful entrepreneur. You have to associate with successful entrepreneurs to get how they think. You have to bring them deeply inside your inner circle. You have to be challenged constantly to break free of your old thinking if you want to be successful as well, particularly in this age of the "new economy of business." — Dr. Ross McKenzie

I've found that entrepreneurs have three common characteristics. First, I look for people who have had an ongoing interest in wanting to come up with solutions to problems. If they're the kind of person who when a challenge is presented to them their mind starts working. That's what entrepreneurship is all about, it's coming up with an idea to solve someone's problem. And then explaining it persuasively enough that they say, "Okay I'm ready to buy in here." So, number one is curiosity and a very strong yen to come up with solutions. Second, I ask "How is this manifested in your life?" Give me a couple examples of how you've been really dedicated to the actual work steps you have to do to make that kind of business succeed. Demonstrated capability. How do we know that you're really good at what you say you want to do here? And third, you've just got to have a lot of confidence in yourself. A lot of what determines your success are what I call serendipity things that just come up to you. You didn't think they were going to happen. If you don't have confidence in yourself, you won't act on these serendipitous events. — Jeffrey Wayman Williams

Failure

Will you do some things wrong in your career and be justly criticized for being unprepared, sloppy, or thoughtless? Sure, you will. When you launch a clunker, the criticism of the failure will be real, but it won't be about you—it'll be about the idea. The greatest artists, playwrights, car designers, composers, advertising art directors, authors, and chefs have all had significant flops—it's part of what makes their successful work great. — Seth Godin

If you try something and it doesn't work, learn from it and move forward again in a different direction. Successful people learn as much from what doesn't work as from what does. Don't be afraid to ask for help. Don't be afraid to admit that you don't know everything. Don't be afraid to surround yourself with others who know different things than you do. There's no shame in failing; at least you tried something new. — Richard Hatheway

Getting Help
Go find a trusted advisor at either the local Small Business Development Center, SCORE or one of the other small business organizations. There is a belief that getting advice is expensive and is unaffordable. These resources are free. Once you are up and running, find a mastermind group to join or start a mastermind group to keep you motivated. — Marc Miller

Launching
When choosing a business, it's helpful to leverage your professional expertise and networks. This doesn't mean you need to continue to do exactly what you were doing as an employee. But if you can do something that is related to your old line of work, you likely will be able to build-up your business faster than if you strike out in a whole new direction. It's also important to connect with other entrepreneurs. Being an entrepreneur can get lonely, so you'll want to find a community of colleagues that can provide support and help with brainstorming and possible business partnership opportunities. — Nancy Collamer

…focus on the expertise and skills [you offer]. Provide strong evidence and examples of what you have done successfully in recent years that would be of interest to the companies or clients you are pursuing. Entrepreneurs who are 50-plus need to think of which problem or problems they can solve for the client rather than thinking, "I need this job" or "Please hire me despite my age." — Richard Eisenberg

Most people don't realize that being an entrepreneur means running a business. This means that you need to be able to handle things like putting up a Web site, handling expenses, getting a logo designed, etc. These are the little things that most people forget about. They just assume that if they are good at certain skills like sales, that everyone will want to hire them. Not true. So, you have to remember that being an entrepreneur means much more than just focusing on your skills, it means understanding and learning how to run an actual business. As you become more successful you can start to build a team that can assist you with these aspects of work. — Jacob Morgan

Marketing

The way you break through to the mainstream is to target a niche instead of a huge market. With a niche, you can segment off a chunk of the mainstream and create an "ideavirus" so focused that it overwhelms that small slice of the market that really and truly will respond to what you sell. The early adopters in this market niche are more eager to hear what you have to say. The system is pretty simple: Go for the edges. Challenge yourself and your team to describe what those edges are (not that you'd actually go there), and then test which edge is most likely to deliver the marketing and financial results you seek. — Seth Godin

Employers are looking for answers across all business functions and in all stages of the business life cycle. And typically, [for] distinctive answers which enable a competitive advantage, power growth or ensure survival. — John Groarke

Make sure you are actively leveraging [project/contract matchmaking] sites and other related platforms to let people know how you can help them. People post thousands of projects they need help with every single day. You need to carve out the time to build your profile so that you look like a credible and respectable professional online. I work with a team of around six freelancers, all of whom I found on [an online platform]. But you need be highly active on these places. Don't just create a profile and then expect the jobs to start flowing in. Especially at the beginning you need to find the projects you want to take on. — Jacob Morgan

Mission

I have often been asked why I gave up a successful corporate career at the age of 50 to start my own business. The simple truth is that I basically woke up one day realising that though I had achieved much, I felt empty and this emptiness was the direct result of not "contributing" to a larger cause or purpose beyond myself and personal needs. Simply, this was a major distinction that has now taken me to new levels to experience what it is to truly be "alive." — Dr. Ross McKenzie

Partnering

I think many times people 50-plus have skills they have performed in Fortune 500 type organizations when they were younger. In a big company you would have narrow specialized skills that have a market. But that same individual may not have the accounting or sales and marketing skills to be able to build and expand a small business. The key is to find people with different but complementary skills who can simulate how a corporation would work. Many skills and needs for a small business can be done by other contractors on an as-needed basis. But for skills that are needed more regularly, partnering can be good. You need a clear understanding of the roles and the income splits up front. Your experience will allow you to connect with people you target. The skills you bring to the table should be well-developed and of value to your potential "partner." —John R. Fugazzie

Positioning

It can be very discouraging for people who think they can't keep up a changing marketplace and position themselves as marketable professionals. I tell people to look back at the last five years of their work. Pick three areas where they can show a strong body of work. What's the common thread? Does it represent an industry or subject area that they've got experience with? Do they speak the language those clients use, the terminology? Can they claim legitimate expertise in that business? They should package those samples and position themselves as specialists with a lot of experience. —Jackie Mathys

Proposals

At the heart of the Qualifications-Based Selection process is the client defining and communicating their overall scope of work (SOW) for the project along with their required and desired qualifications of the professional to achieve their project's objectives. Price is not a consideration until the client selects the most qualified firm or individual. Once the client and professional agree on the SOW, the freelancer then develops and submits a detailed proposal, including the total price for materials, products, travel, services and any other items needed to complete the engagement. Any negotiations on the overall cost of completing the project focus on adjustments to the SOW, not the consultant's hourly fee. — Greg Hansen

Rates

In order to raise your rates, you need to stop being seen as a commodity where you are compared on price. You are not a piece of steel or copper. You are a person with valuable experience. There are three parts to this: (1) Package your offering in such a way that you can't be compared to others and that is a "no brainer" to your ideal client. (2) Have a sales process/funnel that actually allows you to demonstrate your value. Don't just quote your rates. Instead, look to establish their real needs in such a way that they learn more about the problem they want solved, the real causes of it and what the best solution is. You can often charge for this, by the way. (3) Ask who is your ideal client? Identify the people who will get the biggest return on investment for what you do (financially and otherwise) because these are the people who will greatly value your work. Understand that for them price is way down their list of criteria. The most important thing is to have their problem solved in the best and fastest way possible. They simply won't trust somebody who charges too little to get the job done properly. Also, ensure your lead generation strategies help you to reach and get in front of these people by educating them about their problems and opportunities. — Una Doyle

Strategy

In my experience, the most important paradigm shift we need to make, particularly as older workers, is to move away from the idea that we need to find out what the employer's/client's agenda is, and then serve that. The bar is raised on us as we age. We are no longer expected to just be part of the pack. There are plenty of younger and cheaper people who can take directions and execute on projects. Our challenge is to be more strategic and to offer a clear, personal and useful set of solutions that are well-defined, very specific and very quantifiable. We need to walk in to any interview, meeting, networking event or other opportunity with our pitch buttoned up and ready to go. The question is not 'How can I help you?' but 'This is what I provide. Are you interested?' — John Tarnoff

Trends

As more boomers want—and need—to work during retirement, we are seeing a rise in boomer entrepreneurs. But rather than pursuing high-intensity, high-growth ventures, most are working as solopreneurs in lifestyle businesses. According to a 2015 Gallup survey of 2,000 boomers, entrepreneurs 50-plus are primarily choosing to start businesses that enable them to be independent (32%), pursue their interests and passions (27%) or increase their income (24%). — Nancy Collamer

As employers increasingly reduce full-time head count, they will still need to get jobs done. This will mean finding part-timers, consultants and contractors to handle projects for them. Whether people 50-plus will get those assignments depends on their expertise and qualifications. I think it is a sad truth that employers will tend to give technology and social media projects to young people, assuming they have the expertise that older people don't. — Richard Eisenberg

I see more 50+ professionals moving increasingly to the "gig economy," as they have either been made redundant or feel vulnerable that they will be because of their age. In consulting, there is demand for 50+ consultants who have left a big-name firm to branch out on their own, as the client benefits from the same experience but at a considerably reduced rate. — Sharon Melamed

Visibility

I think I'd say that people need to take advantage of the transparency of the modern world and how social media is actually rather meritocratic. If you have a talent, a viewpoint, something interesting to say or a unique way of thinking it, then it's easier to be "discovered" than ever. There is a huge risk of survivorship bias, and this strategy won't work for everyone, but know that the world needs smart people, wise people, people who see change in context. — Tom Goodwin

Vision

Consultancy is the first choice of many, but is this really being an entrepreneur? A contract with a previous employer can help you segue into a consultancy business, but is this truly what you want to do? Take time to be clear on where you see your future. Create a vision for your 60s and beyond and be clear on your success criteria. Not everyone wants a million-dollar business. A lifestyle business may be the right choice for you. As you consider possible options think widely. Whatever the first idea you come up with, think of at least three more and then do some scenario planning. How could each turn out, from the most positive outcome to a more negative one? Consider too the changes in the external environment. How will the impact of AI [artificial intelligence] affect your business idea and what possibilities will open up? Do your research to make sure that you have a good chance of success. Imagine you are facing the dragons/sharks on TV [where entrepreneurs pitch their businesses]. Would your projections stand up to scrutiny? Then try it on. Does it excite you? Are you raring to go? Or, does it feel like a slog? Once you have done your analysis, you will want to look within. Is this where you want to spend your time and energy over the next 10+ years? — Denise Taylor

Your Value

Older, wiser, smarter people, please chip in. Please don't ever think you're not exactly what we need. Don't be intimidated by the talk of change, the buzzwords… raise your hand and join the debate. Embrace the new, see what really has changed. Flex your mobile muscles. Think about what streaming really means. Your instincts are right, your input is needed. Please don't let anyone suggest otherwise. It's now been such a long time that we've completely forgotten what it's like to have someone in the room who objectively knows more. Who, while earning the big bucks (that it's hard to explain to our clients) understands real clients' issues? And who above all else can see the changes in business and marketing in the context of decades of what has happened before? These days we lazily assume that things have changed and their knowledge would be out of date now. What can we possibly learn from someone who may happen to have a 16-

year-old daughter and therefore probably has a more intimate understanding of contemporary behavior than anyone? — Tom Goodwin

Skills, knowledge and experience will always be paramount attributes. But coupling them with insight makes that doubly so. What the 50+ professional brings to his/her employer's table must be relevant to the challenges to be resolved and the opportunities to be realised. — John Groarke

There is a tremendous amount of expertise, experience and perspective stored in the 50+ generations. Not only that, but there is a quality of resilience developed over time and through confrontation of earlier challenges that finds good application in entrepreneurship. Though many individuals over 50 are less technically adept than their younger counterparts, they have valuable abilities that are sometimes in short supply in the less seasoned generations. Older workers are often extensively networked and business savvy, in addition to having deep and broad domain experience. They offer terrific value as mentors, sponsors and consulting strategists. — Whitney Johnson

People don't realize how much they've learned in their careers. It usually goes much deeper than just what appears on their resumes. This rises to the surface when they have the opportunity to describe how their experience translates into what they can do for clients today with little project ramp-up. There's big value in their ability to solve problems from day one. — Jackie Mathys

There is a perception that 50+ professionals are, on average, more stable and reliable. So, if the client has a consulting project which absolutely must be delivered by a certain date, he/she may feel more confident that an older consultant will adhere to the deadline than a younger one. In situations where there is a requirement to engage with the C-suite or board level, a client may feel a "grey-haired suit" is less risky and more culturally aligned than a "blue jeans 20-something." Age 50+ professionals have simply been around longer, so in theory they should have greater depth of experience and more references and testimonials than their younger peers. This builds trust with clients using their services. — Sharon Melamed

You have years of experience and skills, but are these the ones that you wish to continue to use? Age 50+ is a perfect time to get laser sharp on the skills (and abilities) that you enjoy using, taking them from outside work life. Too often, people forget about the skills they have or downplay them, assuming everyone can do something that they find easy. Take time to consider where you are exceptional and how you stand out from other people. — Denise Taylor

Contributor Profiles

Nancy Collamer
Semi-retirement expert, speaker, author, columnist and blogger
Recognized expert on semi-retirement and boomer career trends, with expertise including career reinvention, second-act careers for boomers, semi-retirement and lifestyle friendly career options.
www.MyLifestyleCareer.com
U.S.A.

Una Doyle
Business coach and strategist for creatives, show host, writer
Helping creative services providers to confidently and profitably stand out from the crowd doing work that fills their hearts with pride—without selling their soul.
www.CreativeFlow.tv
United Kingdom

Richard Eisenberg
Managing Editor and Senior Web Editor, Money & Security and Work & Purpose Channels at Next Avenue and author, former Executive Editor at Money magazine and Front Page Finance Editor at Yahoo!
Consumer-service journalism editor, writing and editing for Web, magazines, newspapers and books, as well as writing and producing for TV.
www.nextavenue.org
U.S.A.

John R. Fugazzie, MBA
Founding director, social entrepreneur, Neighbors-helping-Neighbors USA Inc., Adjunct Professor, Executive Director Hudson County Workforce Development Board
One of the country's leading subject matter experts and leaders in workforce, job search training, career education and jobs creation.
www.johnrfugazzie.com
U.S.A.

Seth Godin
Entrepreneur, author and speaker
Author of 18 best-selling books. He writes and speaks about the post-industrial revolution, the way ideas spread, marketing, leadership and most of all, changing everything.
www.sethgodin.com
U.S.A.

Tom Goodwin
EVP, Head of Innovation at Zenith USA, author and speaker
A focus is the intersection of marketing, technology and business to drive business growth.
www.tomfgoodwin.com
U.S.A.

John Groarke
Principal at JEGMC, Senior Partner at FindAConsultant, consultant and mentor
Known as Australia's "Mentor to Consultants," guides clients to breakthrough with relevant, distinctive, focused, sustainable and profitable enterprises.
www.jegmc.com
Australia

Kerry Hannon
Author, keynote speaker and expert columnist
National keynote speaker and a recognized expert strategist on finding work over 50, as well as entrepreneurship, career transitions, retirement and personal finance for women.
www.kerryhannon.com
U.S.A.

Greg Hansen
Principal at GQG Consulting, strategy, marketing and market research services
Facilitates a process for individuals and organizations exploring possibilities, crafting visions, setting goals, and executing strategies to achieve breakthrough results.
www.gqgconsulting.com
U.S.A.

Richard Hatheway
Marketing expert, consultant and entrepreneur
Technology marketing professional, a technology industry veteran and a business owner.
www.slideshare.net/RichardHatheway
U.S.A.

Whitney Johnson
Speaker, author and performance coach
Through writing, speaking, consulting and coaching, she works with leaders to retain their top talent, to build an A team, and to help them be bosses people love.
www.whitneyjohnson.com
U.S.A.

Joseph Liu
Career and personal branding consultant, speaker, podcast host and IFC certified coach
A passion for helping people gain the clarity, confidence and courage to pursue truly meaningful careers, through speaking, coaching and the Career Relaunch Podcast.
www.josephpliu.com
United Kingdom

Jackie Mathys
Co-Founder/COO of MATHYS+POTESTIO and Written Agency
Matching clients with highly specialized, hard-to-find writers, editors, strategists and other editorial experts.
www.mathys-potestio.com and www.writtenagency.com
U.S.A.

Sharon Melamed
Managing Director at Matchboard, AboutMatch and FindAConsultant
After 23 years in sales for global outsourcing companies, founded unique on-line businesses that match buyers and suppliers in different niches.
www.matchboard.com.au, www.aboutmatch.co.uk, www.findaconsultant.com.au
Australia

Dr. Ross McKenzie
Futurist, speaker, mentor and Founder and Chief Executive Officer of The Startup Business
Leading expert authority on new economy business.
www.thestartupbusiness.com
Australia

Marc Miller
Career design specialist and coach, podcaster, author, board member Launch Pad Job Club
Helping baby boomers make career pivots.
www.careerpivot.com
U.S.A.

Jacob Morgan
Best-selling author, keynote speaker and futurist
Explores what the future of work is going to look like and how to create great experiences so that employees actually want to show up to work.
www.thefutureorganization.com
U.S.A.

John Tarnoff
Author, reinvention career coach, speaker and instructor
A reinvention career coach who provides career counseling for baby boomer and late career professionals looking to defy ageism, ignore retirement and pivot to a new job or new business as a second act or encore career.
www.johntarnoff.com
U.S.A.

Denise Taylor
Author, award winning career coach and career management
Amazing People and Chief Inspiration Officer at The50PlusCoach.
www.The50PlusCoach.co.uk
United Kingdom

Joe Wasylyk

Seniorpreneur, author, blogger

Founder of the Seniorpreneur Project, established to find new ways to help seniors (50 plus) achieve higher levels of lifelong learning and enable them to become more active, creative and productive in their retirement years.

www.seniorpreneur.ca

Canada

Jeffrey Wayman Williams

Boomer business startup coach and entrepreneur

Jeff Williams and his network of expert Virtual Incubator coaches have been guiding new boomer business owners since 1992 to plan, launch and grow fun and profitable enterprises.

www.bizstarters.com

U.S.A.

About the Author

Doug Freeman has been a self-employed entrepreneur for over three decades. He co-founded his company Ideascape, Inc. with his wife and fellow entrepreneur, MacKenzie. They recently launched Imaginexxus LLC as a publishing business for their unconventional travel books and products. Doug also co-founded four other startups with partners. These included a book publishing company, business documentary production firm, innovation think tank and entertainment development company.

Over the years, Doug has adapted his services to market trends and personal interests. His work has included all types of technical and non-technical business, marketing, educational, training, public relations, ghostwriting, media development as well as creative and consulting services. He has served clients ranging from NASA, the U.S. Department of Energy, U.S. Department of the Interior and the Armed Forces Network to Intel, Hewlett-Packard, T-Mobile and Southern Company. Additionally, he has worked with scores of startups, small businesses, local government agencies and non-profit organizations.

Doug has earned regional and national awards for his technical writing, video scriptwriting and media productions. These include

Telly Awards, a NASA Achievement Award and a U.S. Department of Energy Exceptional Public Service Award. His award-winning educational videos on entrepreneurship were selected for presentation at film festivals in three countries.

I invite you to share your workarounds and entrepreneurship experiences with me. Perhaps I'll include your story in one of my posts or articles published on LinkedIn, Twitter and Medium. You can contact me via my Web site at www.ideascapeinc.com, LinkedIn at www.linkedin.com/in/dougatideascapeinc and Twitter at twitter.com/ideascapeinc. To keep up on my latest posts and articles, follow me on any of these social network platforms.

www.ingramcontent.com/pod-product-compliance
Lightning Source LLC
Chambersburg PA
CBHW052251220526
45471CB00001B/284